The Gift I Was Given

The Journey of a Caregiver through the Stages of *What Now?*, *Why Me?*, & *Ah Ha!*

By

Mary Anne Ehlert

New York

The Gift I Was Given

The Journey of a Caregiver Through the Stages of What Now?, Why Me?, & Ah Ha!

ISBN 978-1-60037-504-0

Library of Congress Control Number: 2009901639

MORGAN · JAMES
THE ENTREPRENEURIAL PUBLISHER

Morgan James Publishing, LLC
1225 Franklin Ave., STE 325
Garden City, NY 11530-1693
Toll Free 800-485-4943
www.MorganJamesPublishing.com

In an effort to support local communities, raise awareness and funds, Morgan James Publishing donates one percent of all book sales for the life of each book to Habitat for Humanity. Get involved today, visit **www.HelpHabitatForHumanity.org**.

What our Readers are Saying

"Mary Anne's passion, life experiences, and business background combine in a unique way to provide a truly practical process to help families with special needs find the peace of mind they are looking for.

It is a must read for anyone who has found him or herself responsible for the care of a child, adult or parent with a disability."

David Bach, #1 New York Times bestselling author, *Start Late, Finish Rich and Fight For Your Money.*

"Anyone that has experienced the true joy, courage and honesty that comes from knowing an individual with intellectual disabilities also comes to know the importance of maximizing your abilities and planning for the future. Mary Anne's experiences throughout her life have given her a unique perspective on how much everyone is alike and how much of a need there is to be prepared to deal with each individuals needs. She is committed to making a difference for others and this book is just one of the ways she strives for that objective."

Doug Snyder, President, Special Olympics, Illinois

"Mary Anne and I grew up in families with disability. We had parents, siblings and relatives that struggled to gain access to the classroom and the workplace. However, today's families want their children with lifelong disabilities to be full citizens and to have access to the for m al economy. Mary Anne's legacy is laying the groundwork for future generations with disability to become part of the financial mainstream. We know there is no single policy issue that captures the promise of existing civil and human rights as does the emerging field of asset development for individuals with disabilities. Mary Anne's story is her legacy – people with disabilities need planning so they too can be part of the American Dream."

Johnette T. Hartnett, Ed.D., Director of Research, National Disability Institute

"The eight step process created by Mary Anne and delivered through Protected Tomorrows has been the single most important ingredient we have used in working with our families developing life care plans for their children. It is simple, understandable, and the process allows the family to focus on what is needed for their child. It also allows a systematic approach to dealing with complex issues. With this process, the value that is delivered to the family is immeasurable. Thank you, Mary Anne."

John R. James, Licensed Advocate for Protected Tomorrows ®

This book is dedicated to my sister Marcia.

She taught me everything that really matters in life.

Contents

Acknowledgments   xi

Introduction to the Journey   1

Adjustments: The Twins   12

Family Perspectives   23

Family Obligations & Hard Decisions   40

Legacy of Marcia   49

Caregiving as a Stepmother The Gifts Applied to Real Life   54

Caregiving as a Daughter The Oldest Daughter's Duty   61

The Gifts Revisited   71

The Eight Steps to Protected Tomorrows   74

Acknowledgments

I wish to thank my siblings, Jim, Ron, Arlene, and Debbie, for sharing with me how Marcia impacted their lives. Their honesty and openness allowed me to put into perspective my memories and experiences with Marcia. I thank my parents, Helen and Roy, for giving Marcia the ability to be the best she could be and encouraging us to do the same with our lives.

And I thank my stepsons for accepting me as their mother and teaching me that being a caregiver is the best job in the whole world.

The Gift I Was Given

Introduction to the Journey

"I can't seem to go on with my life without Marcia. I know I must, but how can one say it is easier as time goes on?"

~ Helen Wallace, Marcia's mother, in an unsent letter to Mary Anne, discovered seven years after Marcia's death.

It hasn't always been easy to get up in front of a crowd and tell my story about my younger sister Marcia, who was born with cerebral palsy. One of the most important times I attempted to share a personal memory of her with others was at her funeral. I was forty-three; she was thirty-nine. The ceremony was in our neighborhood Catholic church in Des Plaines, where we had gone to services, and to school, all of our lives. My brothers and sisters had already told their stories. I thought they had done a really nice job at sharing their memories. When it came to be my turn to speak, I anxiously stood to tell an endearing story about our family vacation on the lake when Marcia was fifteen. As I stood in the front of the church, I looked out at my friends and family facing me, most with tears streaming down their faces. Many of them had heard me share my adventures with Marcia before, but this time was different. I had suspected that this time, it would be much more difficult to tell a story, but I had no idea just how hard it would really be. I had even prepared some notes, which I normally don't need.

I thought I had better be prepared with a little backup. As I opened my mouth—as well as my heart—to begin my story, only tears came. I couldn't find any words that were sufficient to honor Marcia and the difference she had made in my life and the lives of those staring up at me. I just stood there and sobbed. This is the story I wanted to tell.

My whole family had gone to my Aunt Virginia's summer home on the lovely up-country lake, Lake Koshkonong, in Wisconsin. This was a very special trip for us, as our family didn't take vacations when we were young. When a family has six children, many financial obligations, and one child with some specific special needs, vacations are not always high on the priority list. We used to consider a day at the local beach as our big, annual outing. So this outing was very special: not only were we actually going somewhere new, but we were staying there overnight! This was going to be a rare treat.

One of our favorite activities was swimming and playing in the cool, clear waters of the lake. The whole family—my parents, Helen and Roy, and their six children: Marcia and Debbie (she was Marcia's identical twin), who were eighteen; Arlene, who was twenty; Ron, who was twenty-four; Jim, who was twenty-seven; and me, at the age of twenty-two—had donned bathing suits, including Marcia. It was a hot day—a typical sticky, humid Chicago summer. The lake was inviting and beautiful. We couldn't wait to dive into the cool water where our six cousins were already frolicking. Now came the first challenge: The lake house was a rustic, two-story, six-room cabin sitting in a wonderfully wooded area at the top (uh-oh!) of a steep hill. The lake itself was situated *way* down at the bottom of the hill. As we looked down the decrepit staircase descending to the shore, we realized that traversing those fifty thousand steps (or so it seemed) was going to be a challenge of monumental proportions. But it was a familiar challenge, one we had faced many times before. My mother and I each took one of Marcia's arms. We trundled down the fifty rickety wooden steps, making sure with each step that Marcia didn't topple over. If you have never helped a person with a physical disability traverse a set of narrow, steep stairs, it may be difficult to appreciate the time and effort this can take. Those of us without a physical disability run up and down stairs regularly without a care in the world. But to us, this ritual with Marcia of "one step at a time" until we reached the bottom was just the status quo.

It was extremely slow going. We finally made it down to the lakeside, where my family and cousins were gathered at the end of a low wooden pier on the shore, waiting in the sweltering heat to help Marcia get in the water. As always, Marcia was the first one in. As she was lowered from the pier, she issued "instructions" for all of us: "Hurry up! Get in the water! Quit being babies!" she chided good-naturedly. As always, Marcia was in charge!

We were swimming, having a great time playing and splashing, always including Marcia in our antics. This was one activity where we were on equal footing. Because the water buoyed Marcia, she could stand alongside us. After an hour of us playing and whooping it up, my father grew cold and decided it was time for him to get out. He swam to the pier, past Marcia, who was standing in the shallow water, enjoying the relief that the cool lake brought from the stifling heat and humidity. With Marcia behind him, my father placed his hands firmly on the steamy wood planks and gave his body a hefty lift out of the lake. Up he came, and off came his signature baggy, mustard yellow bathing suit, brought down to his knees by the rush of water. Moon shot!

Standing right behind him, Marcia witnessed the whole thing. She couldn't contain herself; she shouted and then laughed and laughed and laughed. Marcia's laughter was always loud, and along with the laughter came her arms thrown way up in the air, to emphasize her delight in the situation. Surprised and extremely embarrassed, my father fell back into the lake. By this time, everyone was aware of what had happened, because Marcia made sure of it. But my father wasn't laughing—at first.

He took several seconds in the water to somberly readjust his suit, and then he pulled himself up to get out again. Another moon shot! *This* one he did on purpose, just to entertain Marcia, who couldn't stop laughing. None of us could, including Dad, because Marcia's laughter, so honest and true, rang out across the lake and infected all of us. In its truth and honesty, Marcia's laughter had stripped away all pretenses and revealed the essential truth to us: we loved being with each other as a family, and we also loved making Marcia laugh.

I knew everyone in my family would fondly remember this story. The recollection would make many of us smile. The story epitomized Marcia, with her contagious laughter, her arms flying up in the air as she laughed, her bossy ways, my family's constant attempts to make the world happy for her. I thought it would be the perfect memory to share. But as funny as this story was, I couldn't tell it at the funeral. The pain of the loss of my sister was too great. I already missed her laughter.

I couldn't imagine her gone from my life. I just stood at the podium and cried.

A week later, I was to try again. I attended a conference where I was to give a speech explaining how I started my business and why I had chosen to focus my practice on families with individuals with disabilities. I thought for sure I was ready this time. I had even practiced my presentation and had prepared even more detailed notes than before. I was determined to get through this. I asked my parents to come along for moral support. I made sure I rehearsed several times at the last minute. But I still could not get through my speech. I stood, again, in front of a crowd and cried. I stumbled through my speech, trying to gather my thoughts, but the words kept getting caught in my throat, and the tears streamed down my face. As I walked down from the stage, mortified, I wondered if it would always be this way. Would I always cry whenever I tried to talk about Marcia?

Over the years, I continued to give speeches, attempting to share my stories about Marcia, each time working very hard to complete them, if at all. The sadness I felt seemed at times to be an overwhelming barrier. Marcia was my teacher and my life's inspiration. All my speeches revolved around her. If I couldn't talk about her, I wondered, how I could continue teaching families with special-needs members? Searching for answers, I knew somehow that Marcia was still with me. I could feel her presence every time I tried to find a new solution for a family. I could feel her all around me every time I did something that we used to do together. When I wrapped Christmas presents, I knew she was there holding the tape for me, like she had always done. When I did something silly, I could still hear her recriminations. I felt her determination when I struggled. I often heard her one-of-a-kind laughter coming through in a crowd. I just knew she was with me somehow. I kept feeling that she was steering me toward some mission and bigger purpose that I did not yet understand. I struggled to find clarity in her message to me. Finally, I decided it was time to use the strength she gave me to reexamine what I had learned from her. After a time, I was able to distill those reflections into "gifts" I had received.

When I first described these gifts to others, many of my friends asked me what made these gifts different than the memories and lessons we all receive from our family members, especially memories from those who have passed before us. I have had to refine my thinking to understand why Marcia's life had such an immense impact on me. The uniqueness was the dependency we had *on each other*. I find this type of dependency in many relationships when one has the responsibility to care for another. There is more than a one-way caring: it is not only a need to *be* cared for but develops into a need *to care for*. This often drives and focuses the caregiver's life.

These gifts are on a list I keep with me always. It is the focus for my life. It is what helps me appreciate life every day. It has helped me face new difficulties in my life with grace. It has made it possible for me to speak of Marcia with love and honor, but seldom with outward tears. *Now* each time I tell the story of my life with Marcia, I smile as I relive and treasure the time I had with her—in joy.

Equally as important as the memories of Marcia are these gifts she left me. I have learned, and continue to relearn, from having lived with a sister with a disability. Perhaps the foremost lesson among these things I have learned is that there is no neutral or detached ground in a family with a member who has disabilities; that is, as I have learned over and over through the years, without exception, every family member is impacted in his or her own unique way by that person's disability (or, more appropriately, that person's unique *abilities*.).

For my family, living with Marcia was the way things were, the status quo, standard operating procedure. My sister, brothers, and I did not know any other way to be with each other. We took all the things that were different about life with Marcia in stride as normal. We loved her devotedly. She was truly the energetic center of our family. The truth is that each of us was an individual with unique gifts to offer and with unique needs to be filled. As I have learned from my own family's experiences, we have coped with Marcia's disabilities and abilities in our own ways and in our own times. We have each been taught invaluable lessons that none of us anticipated.

I have been asked by those friends and associates of mine who were not lucky enough to have experienced my sister (or another person with a disability) in their lives what makes my life any different than theirs. After all, they, too, were molded by their families. Those who have been a caregiver of a person with a disability don't ask the same questions, as they, too, have been on the road that requires taking a slightly different path. I do feel now that I am on a spiritual journey. I am fully aware of the grace that surrounds me. I truly believe I would not have been able to maintain a sense of any purpose in my life if Marcia had not been there with me. I look at life differently now. What is even more unique for me is the number of times I have already been challenged to have faith and to be there as a caregiver for others. Why me? I cannot tell you. But I have been given this job many times. For some reason, Marcia was in my life to prepare me for what was to come.

The gifts Marcia left me prepared me for this future of caregiving. Without the core values and the courage to understand each of the responsibilities I was given, I don't believe I could have made it through each of these opportunities with grace. I call them "opportunities" because Marcia helped me find my place, find my way, and find my purpose. I define "grace" as the innate sense that things are happening around me for a reason. I just need to listen carefully, be aware of them, and accept them into my life, doing the best I can. Many of us take a lifetime to be able to experience something that allows us to put our lives in perspective. I think perhaps I was an "old soul" before my time. The experience and wisdom Marcia was able to impart to me at a relatively young age prepared me for the jobs I was to assume in the years to come. I consider every lesson Marcia taught me to be a gift, and I hope to share those gifts with you so that Marcia's life continues to have purpose in the world we live in.

Goals and Hopes

Looking back on my caregiving journey so far, it was not a straight path, nor did it have any type of planned itinerary. I am a planner by nature. I like to know where I am going, how I will get there, and when I will arrive. My destination and the route I will take are always preplanned. But as I look at this journey, it is only through hindsight that I see the value this journey has had on my life. Though at times an emotional and extremely trying journey, it was a necessary one in order for me to understand the true nature of relationships. And there was no straight route. I went through the many paths again and again and in no particular order. You would think I would have learned the first time, wouldn't you? But it is the nature of learning that we need to assimilate our experiences differently each time in order to define the clear path for the future.

Over time, I gave the different stopping points a name, so that at least I would understand where I was. The point of "What Now?" was typically the entry point at which I was entering a new stage of my journey. I did not know what was in store for me, and I didn't know where to begin or even from where to get direction. I felt confused and unclear as to the next steps. The point of "Why Me?" was the path on which I was feeling totally alone and unsupported. I felt I was totally responsible. Why couldn't someone else step in to take responsibility? Why did I have to have more of this in my life? But the final leg of each journey always had the "Ah Ha!" for me, where it all came together. I could see why I was where I was and actually felt blessed to be on the particular path I was on. I could see the destination and appreciated it.

My first goal in writing this book is to share the lessons I learned through living with Marcia. Connecting them to meaningful stories about Marcia's life makes them truly useful and not just quotes to hang on the wall, but words that I hope will instill in others the same hope and wonder that she instilled in me. Perhaps through *my* lessons, others will learn to appreciate the journeys *they* are on.

I've built an advocacy company, which started in 1989 as a career as a certified financial planner, with a specialty in planning for families with children with disabilities. When I first started out working with families to help with this necessary life planning, many other advisors told me that there were just not enough families to serve; the audience I wanted to reach was too small. But I was driven by the fact that Marcia lived with cerebral palsy. I heard the fears my parents had verbalized to me about who would be there for Marcia when they were gone, and this directed me into financial planning for families having members with special needs. Little did I realize at that time that, according to the US census, there were over 53.9 million individuals with disabilities in the United States alone. They needed much more than financial planning. They needed an advocate to help them find resources, including appropriate schools, residences, work, and play. Marcia's influence has played a vital role in the success of my practice. As I continued to search out solutions, the need kept growing. It is an international issue, not just in any one city or country. I have focused on applying to my work the primary touchstones, or values, Marcia taught me—about what's important in life, about how to be myself in the world, and about how to relate to others. Those gifts remain the bedrock from which my life is built.

Another goal is to let parents know that the lives of the other siblings are *better*, not *burdened*, as a result. Thousands of parents have expressed to me how they felt that they had "cheated" their other children from a "normal" childhood. I am here to tell them that most of us feel we are better off as people. Our sibling with a disability has had a profound and significant positive impact on our lives.

Being a sister of a sibling with a disability, I've become fascinated with the siblings' perspectives on having a brother or sister with special needs. I understand the unique relationship we shared, and yet I know it was unlike the relationship Marcia had with our parents. Generally speaking, the parents carry the burden of the future's uncertainties, the worry, and the heartache of the disability. They also have the challenge of raising their other children in the special-needs environment. Siblings, on the other hand, generally don't worry or see the disability as a burden in the same way. Wheelchairs, medications, seizures, drooling, and unusual exercises end up not being unusual at all but just part of the daily tenor and routine … normal for the family.

In my work with families with individuals with disabilities, I see the relationships among all the members of the family. Parents often feel uncertain about how and who to leave the responsibility of future care to. Parents feel that they should not have to place this burden on those who were already impacted in their family, but they also know they must. I want to emphasize that children who have siblings with disabilities do not all feel cheated. On the contrary, many of us feel blessed to have had the family that we did. And we are ready and willing to pass on those blessings. We are ready to commit ourselves to becoming Future Care People, as I call them, people who make the future safe for persons with disabilities, but we also want to be provided with some directions and guidance.

I'd like to relay information and provide guidance to families of individuals with disabilities and to alert them to the importance of looking forward, for the well-being of the whole family. Parents focus primarily on the child with special needs in the present, not on planning for future care or financial stability. Parents may ask, "What will our lives be like in the future?" but then a more immediate need concerning their child arises, and planning for the future is interrupted. To assist in formulating plans that assure no family members will be burdened with unmanageable costs or expectations, I will share with you my own personal process for setting up life plans, as well as financial plans, just as I did for Marcia and my parents.

Another goal is to help all caregivers find a sense of peace. I learned some important lessons from Marcia. As I continued on with my life after her death, I was faced with several new challenges. Each time I unwrapped the gifts Marcia gave me, I applied their lessons, and each time, they formed the basis for a particular aspect of inner peace. I will admit that there were still very difficult times ahead, and I struggled through each one, but I am more convinced than ever that Marcia has been by my side all along the way on these journeys.

My final goal is that this book will be able to go where I cannot. I have a busy career running my business and a full schedule of speaking engagements, and I cannot always be where I am needed, nor can I always fully and completely explain or describe the impact Marcia has had on my life. With this book, the message of Marcia's life in its entirety can reach many more families and individuals in need than I could ever reach alone.

Apart from these goals, I would also like to share one other gift I was given: hope. Hope filled our family. Life with Marcia was truly a life full of hope. I would like to give each family a vision of hope for their family member and for themselves. Hope has given me the drive to always feel that when things appear impossible, there is always a solution. The bigger the problem seems, the more important it is to be creative in finding the answers. Most importantly, Marcia left me with a passion—a passion to want to make a difference and to find solutions to even the hardest of life's problems.

Of course, multiple siblings in a family will inevitably have different perspectives and feelings about the sibling with the disability. Experiences and feelings change as the siblings grow and change through childhood, adolescence, young adulthood, and adulthood. I am fortunate to have two other sisters, one of whom is Marcia's identical twin, who were willing to share their own unique perspectives on how life with Marcia changed them. I am equally as fortunate to have two older brothers who loved Marcia deeply but, for their own reasons, were unable to share, at the time I was writing this book, their experiences in detail.

I have been blessed by the impact that Marcia's life had on me and my brothers and sisters as we took on the responsibility for our parents' care in their later years. I will share with you the ways in which Marcia prepared us for many obstacles that we otherwise may not have been able to confront with the grace that we did. I do believe that Marcia was there with us in many ways as we took on the responsibilities we faced as caregivers in many other areas of our lives.

It has taken over ten years since Marcia's death for me to share with others my journey and the gifts I have received. I felt that if I kept them to myself, I could keep Marcia closer to me, but time has taught me that she would want me to share her gifts, for it is through sharing that her life continues to make a difference. It is my hope that somewhere in these recollections from the five of us, and from the innumerable lessons we have learned, others will find threads of similarity to their own lives. And the hope that their lives, too, can be filled with the joy that our family felt on a daily basis.

Thank you, Marcia.

Adjustments:

The Twins

"When the twins were born and I was told the one had a problem, I wondered how I could cope. But somehow I did, we all did!"

~ Helen Wallace

I was a month shy of four when my mother had the twins. I don't remember much about the events surrounding their births. My little sister was only one and a half and didn't know any family life without them. All I recall is that my mother had to go away for a few days, so my cousin Patsy stayed with the four of us. We had fun with Patsy while we waited for Mom to come home. When she did, we learned that we had two brand-new sisters.

What my parents knew and experienced was a whole different story. Marcia had been born first but with complications. The umbilical cord had wrapped around her neck. The time it took the doctors to disentangle Marcia from the cord was enough time without oxygen for her to sustain brain damage. Debbie was born minutes later, amazingly healthy and crying.

Cerebral palsy doesn't always show itself right away in an infant. The developmental delays, both physical and intellectual, can take several months to become apparent. So when my parents brought the girls home, there was no diagnosis and no apparent concern. They were our two perfect, identical little sisters.

As the twins grew, Debbie gained weight, increased her movement and muscle control, began to babble and coo—all the things a typically progressing baby does. Marcia, on the other hand, began to show signs of delay. Her arms and legs lacked muscle tone and strength. She clenched her tiny hands so tightly that her little knuckles turned white. When Debbie started pushing herself up with her arms, Marcia still lay on her back staring at unknown things on the ceiling. At first, my parents, especially Dad, simply said that Marcia would catch up. "Don't worry," Dad kept saying to us, even as the differences became more pronounced. Young as we were, we believed anything our father said. We knew Marcia would be okay.

Marcia *would* be okay, but the physical and mental impairments brought about by the cerebral palsy would dictate that her life path diverge significantly from mine and from our sisters'.

My parents were very optimistic and devoutly religious people. When my mother was pregnant with me, after having had two boys, she said the rosary every day so that I'd be a girl. She got her wish. (Throughout my childhood, she told me this story every time I acted like a tomboy! If I was playing roughhouse with my brothers, she said, "I prayed for a girl, but look at you! You are all dirty, running around like a boy!") Why shouldn't anything they tried with regard to

Marcia get the same results? Accordingly, my parents prayed for her. They taught us to add to our prayers each night the wish that Marcia would catch up. Our family tenor abounded with positive thoughts, uplifting ideas, and positive action. Within the edifice of my parents' optimism, though, was a self-induced blindness, an unwillingness to see Marcia's delays for what they were. My father, in particular, refused to accept any disability as permanent. There was always the uncritical expectation that she would eventually catch up.

I have learned over time that this delay in acceptance is a normal part of life. It takes us time to accept those things that will alter the dreams we have for the future. But the learning process cannot begin until we face reality. We must take a candid look at where we really are and see with open eyes what our future might hold.

The babies continued to grow, but even as identical twins, they began to look and act differently. Debbie maintained a typical progression of development—sitting, standing, and learning to walk—as if on cue. Marcia also grew, but she learned everything more slowly. She seemed not to be fully *in* her body and could not control it the way she wanted. From the beginning, though, and despite the frustration of having misbehaving appendages, Marcia showed an extraordinary ability to infect others with her laughter. It was a pure, clear, giddy note that resonated through our rooms like a chime and that incited us to join her. As she grew, we learned that Marcia was incapable of preventing herself from being honest. In the years to come, this trait, along with her humor, proved to be a support upon which many of our family's decisions were made.

When Marcia's delays became more and more apparent, my parents finally moved fully into solution mode. Trips to doctors brought more information and ideas on treatment; trips to the library revealed alternative therapy options. My parents investigated every avenue of hope they encountered in the faith that one of them would assist Marcia to progress beyond her limited state. With the help that they were providing her, they believed that she would catch up, and armed with that faith, they were steadfast in their pursuit of treatment.

Little by little, Marcia became the center of the family structure. The family began to operate as a unit to take care of her and help her progress. None of us children questioned what we did or why. We just did what we needed to do to make sure our sister Marcia could continue to play with us and make us laugh. Didn't every family have someone like Marcia in their lives? Wasn't this normal? Weren't we all individuals and unique in our own ways, after all? Gradually, though, I, along with my brothers and other sisters, began to wonder if maybe Dad was wrong about Marcia being able to catch up to Debbie. Maybe Marcia *was* different from the rest of us. Maybe she *wasn't* going to catch up—ever. But Dad remained adamant that Marcia would improve—adamant, that is, until the day he and my mother took Marcia in for an evaluation and the doctor came back with a diagnosis.

There are rare moments that rise above all others in the expanse of landscape we call our lives. Weddings, births, and deaths come to mind as being representative of such moments. They define us in ways that capture the essence of who we are, what our dreams are, and why we grieve. Like the ancient milestones that measured the distance from Rome, they measure the distance from the heart. Those moments, in turn, become beacons that guide us home. Such a moment came for my parents when our doctor called them into the examination room where he had been administering a battery of neurological tests to Marcia. The doctor said, in a voice more sorrowful than solemn—he knew from clinical experience what his diagnosis would mean— "Your daughter has cerebral palsy."

"Cerebral palsy," he went on to say, "is a group of chronic conditions affecting body movement and muscle coordination. This is a developmental disability caused by damage to one or more specific motor areas of the brain. There are no problems in the muscles or nerves themselves, but the damage to the brain disrupts the brain's ability to adequately control movement and posture. The disability is not a disease: it's not communicable; it is not progressive. There are management systems available involving specialized training and therapy that help control muscle movement. And," he added finally, "there is no cure."

There! The delays were spelled out, the changing body explained.

Armed with this diagnosis, both my mother and my father departed the doctor's office relieved to finally have something concrete to work with and determined to investigate every single one of the specialized trainings and therapies the doctor had mentioned. They vowed to themselves that through their family's hard work and sacrifice and their faith in God, their Marcia would be the exception who proved the prognosticators wrong. They researched the topic of cerebral palsy where they could: libraries, medical journals, newspapers. They made countless phone calls. They talked to innumerable specialists. But after the initial shock of the diagnosis had worn off, and after all their research had provided them with precious little to go on apart from their own faith, the reality of Marcia's condition and what it *really* meant for her and for us gradually began to sink in. I can't say I remember the exact moment when my parents did finally come to accept Marcia's disability as a permanent condition. It seemed to me that they came to this realization only gradually, and only very, *very* grudgingly. In other words, they never had an "ah ha!" moment of knowing, but grew accustomed to the situation bit by bit before they finally accepted the reality. Their daughter Marcia was a person with a disability, and she would have this disability for the rest of her life.

So began my parents' lifelong journey to find the best treatments and the best therapies. They stopped at nothing to seek out the most innovative approaches to help their daughter live the fullest and best life she could. This became their purpose, and if there was an inkling of hope anywhere, they searched it out.

Sometime after the age of two, Marcia learned how to walk, but only with a lot of help. I can remember starting my "new job" as big sister then. I was only six, but I would hold her hand to steady her, or brace her from behind, to help her to walk. Knowing that I was there if she should fall gave Marcia confidence. She responded with delight and enthusiasm at her newfound abilities. Our family had adapted to living with Marcia's delayed abilities. She was always slower than we were, but that was just a fact. Everyone was different, so it really didn't matter.

But then Marcia started having seizures.

That's when life for our family changed significantly—and forever. With this milestone in the progression of Marcia's cerebral palsy, we all became aware at once, and in our own ways, of the singular fragility of life. This would be the first time that we as children would witness something that seemed unnatural and beyond any understanding of the world. Till then, we had been sheltered by our parents from this unknown part of life that seemed to defy any rational explanation. After all, the job of parents is to insulate their children from the harsh realities that young minds are not yet ready to fathom. Our parents had done their job probably better than most. After Marcia started having seizures, there was nothing that could protect us from the stark reality that our sister Marcia's experiences had been, and were likely to be for a long time, far different from our own.

I can remember clearly the first time she had a seizure. It is interesting that when I asked my sisters to write their recollections about Marcia we all recalled this event vividly and almost exactly the same. Although we each remember many different stories, this one particular event was embedded in each of our brains as a major event in our lives. We were all quite young, so to remember this day in the detail we do is amazing. We each clearly remember this life-changing event only *slightly* differently, yet it impacted every one of us forever in unique ways.

Our childhood home had a large combined living and dining room. A big, black, baby grand piano (which was even bigger to us than it was in real life) divided the two rooms. As large as it was, under the piano was a safe and cozy haven for us to play with our dolls. Mom was in the kitchen preparing dinner, just as she did every late afternoon. Something fell from her hands and crashed to the floor with a loud noise. It was a sound that would reverberate through our lives.

Marcia became startled and jumped at the sound. Then, she started trembling. Her eyes grew glazed and unfocused. Her mouth twitched. Tears ran from her eyes. She wasn't able to explain to us what was happening. She became incoherent, she began to drool, and then she began throwing up all over the floor.

Frightened as never before, because we had never witnessed anything like it, we dropped our dolls and started screaming for our mother. She could fix almost anything and, more than anything else in the world, we wanted her to come and make Marcia stop shaking.

At our screams, Mom rushed in. She took Marcia in her arms and spoke softly to her, assuring her and us that everything would be all right. After a few minutes Marcia did grow quiet. We *knew* Mom could make things right. But we were shaken and absolutely frightened by the incident. We wanted only for her to make things better. None of us wanted our sister to have this problem. Later in life, I learned that Mom was just as frightened as we were on that day, even though, at that time, she made us feel very safe that things would go back to normal.

We all helped bathe Marcia, for she had become incontinent during the episode. Mom called my father at work to come home and take Marcia to see our doctor. At the emergency room of the hospital, the doctor explained to my parents what had happened, and he prescribed medications that might help.

That day was a fork in the road for each of us and would influence the paths that the rest of our lives would take. I can still sense the uncertainty of that day as though it were yesterday. After that, we all felt some trepidation every time we played under the piano. To this day, I have the big, black, baby grand piano in my home, and even though it didn't fit into several of my homes, I just kept moving it and squeezing it in somewhere. For some reason, I just couldn't part with it. I didn't realize until this writing why it is so important to keep that piano in my life: It provides a memory, or a milestone, marking the distance to the heart of the one event that started me on the path I have taken as a caregiver.

I find it even more interesting to see how that one day started each of us on very different paths that we might not otherwise have taken. What would my sisters' lives be like now if this day had not occurred as it had? Arlene described that day much as I had, except that she recalled her role as being the one who cleaned up the vomit on the floor by herself, being very proud of that accomplishment. It was the very first time she recalled wanting to be a nurse. Today Arlene *is* a nurse. Debbie (Marcia's twin) didn't recall the event with the same detail, since she was younger, but she says it was then that she recognized that our family was different. This event made her "think about life more than the average bear," as she puts it. Although very young, she started thinking, even *then*, about how we got here, where we go when we die, who God is, and why everyone is different. To this day, she remains on a passionate search, looking desperately for these answers. I am absolutely convinced that the day Marcia had her first seizure was the intersection in my life from which I set out on the road to being a caregiver. If I ask anyone today for one word that describes my life, "caregiver" is the word they most often use, because I have cultivated from that day forward my innate ability to keep others safe and have turned it into my life's work. From my own experience and that of my sisters, it becomes clearer to me each and every day that Marcia set us all on our life paths more than anyone or anything else. I would like to believe that the gifts the three of us have learned to bestow on others are as beneficial and as freely given as were Marcia's gifts to us. It is a tall order to fill, but with Marcia as our example, we have a beacon to guide us. With it, I do not see how we can ever lose sight of the road.

As the seizures continued, the family made adjustments .We all learned quickly how to help Marcia be safe and comfortable whenever they occurred. Marcia was embarrassed by her seizures, in part because she would wet her pants. She came to hate these episodes. "They make me feel like a baby," she would say, articulating her thoughts clearly. Sometimes, she could tell us when one was coming, and she would prepare us for it, while at other times, they came out of the blue. In any case, we would just hold her and speak softly to console her, as our mother had taught us, because there was nothing else we could do until the seizure had run its course. We eventually learned that we didn't have to take Marcia to the emergency room every time she had a seizure. The hospital only sent us home each time. There wasn't anything they could do that we couldn't do at home ourselves. For me, the hardest part of the seizures was waiting helplessly for them to end. Although I knew more or less what caused them, I still didn't like seeing my sister in the grip of her misfiring brain. I prayed every night that the violent convulsions, the loss of control, and the dreadful toll that the spasms took on my sister and my family would cease and never return. Mostly, though, it was the monumental unfairness of it all that made me want to understand how I could do more to help her. *Why*, I asked myself many, many times, *can't I do more?*

When my friends now ask me how my life was different, and why I think my sister's life changed me more than their siblings may have impacted their own, here is where it is *very clear* to me. Unless you become a caregiver as a very young child, how do you understand the compelling need to fix things so much that it drives many of your life's decisions? The need to make things okay becomes a part of you.

Each of the bouts of seizures would end eventually. Each time,

Marcia would sleep for hours. Then, peace did come to her. We all went about the various cleaning chores we were assigned. There was no feeling among us of being put upon. No question in our minds as to what our duties were. The most memorable feeling was one of relief that Marcia was out from under the grip of the seizure.

As she grew older, we found that loud noises could trigger her seizures. This fact affected all of us and many of our activities. If Marcia became startled because of a sudden noise and sudden activity, a seizure could be the result. So when it came to playing games, all of us kids had to be cautious about not whooping and yelling when we won the game. Mom had to be aware of where Marcia was in the house when she turned on the vacuum cleaner or used the blender. As children, was this our main focus? No. Did we still play like any other kids? Yes, but with an awareness that we needed to pay a little more attention. Did this seem strange to us? No. It was just the way it was.

We did learn the importance of being prepared. Marcia could have a seizure anywhere, at any time. Just as a family is prepared with diapers and wipes, extra clothes, and toys when taking out an infant, we were prepared when going out with Marcia. This became part of our routine. *Nothing unusual.*

As I look back, I recognize we also had some opportunities as children that we might not have had if not for Marcia. For instance, we always had a pool in our backyard, since swimming was good therapy for Marcia. And over the years, as Marcia got older, the pool also got bigger. We knew the pool was special; it was a luxury we had specifically for Marcia. It was just something we needed to have in our family. *Nothing unusual.*

So we all became settled into life, as it was, with Marcia. I can remember playing in the front yard one day, at a time when Marcia, with our help, could still walk a little and was able to play with us outside. Something once again surprised her that day—a backfire, a tree branch snapping, a dog barking, something—and she fell hard to the sidewalk, which was uneven and with treacherous footing. Bright red blood streamed from her head and seeped into the cracks where she had hit the concrete. Soon there was blood everywhere. Being children, none of us had ever seen anything like it before. We were petrified. I was sure that my sister was critically ill. I finally ran to tell my mother what had happened. Since Mom didn't drive, she called our cousin Patsy, who came to take Marcia and my mother to the emergency room. When it was all over, Marcia proudly showed us the stitches that closed the wound on her head. It healed soon, but things were never the same after that. For us, the trauma of going through this experience set a new stage. We all knew we would have to be just a little more careful, because the consequences could be too great if we were not.

For example, there used to be occasions when Marcia would be left alone in a room or outside while we were playing, and we didn't think anything of it. I recall that I once left Marcia for a short time to get a drink in the kitchen. When I returned, I discovered that she had begun to have a seizure, probably in response to a loud noise. I felt guilty for having left the room and vowed to try to never be that irresponsible again, even though I knew it probably would have happened if I had been in the room or not. But I still felt responsible. Nobody blamed me, of course, but events such as this reinforced over and over in me a sense of personal responsibility, one that developed hand in hand with what I felt had become my duty: to care for others. Moreover, from the vantage of the present, I am able to see that this sense of responsibility, coupled with my self-imposed obligation to be Marcia's and my parents' caregiver, has brought me full circle both in my personal life and in my career. To this day, I consider responsibility a reward in my life.

Debbie shared a similar story with me. She recalled a time when she and Marcia were ten-year-olds and they were outside playing. By that age, Marcia needed assistance when walking, or she could fall. A bee buzzed Debbie. Her natural instinct had been to run away from the bee in order to avoid being stung. She had run a few yards away from Marcia when she realized she had left her behind, and then she ran back immediately. For the last forty-one years, she has thought about that event as being an eye-opener to her about the nature of responsibility. Like me, she had learned a lesson that day that could not be put fully into words, because, unlike obligations, which are known primarily through the mind, the sense of responsibility comes mostly from the heart. Its actions are known mostly through the care we extend to others.

The seizures were just one aspect of Marcia's disability that moved her into the center of the family structure. In truth, most of our family activities revolved around Marcia. Her laughter was usually quite loud and noticeable. When she laughed, her arms always went up in the air, and by this gesture, everyone knew that she was about to begin a round of laughter. If we went someplace where loud laughter was "out of vogue," we tried to prepare her and give her hints how she could "laugh softly." Of course, her spontaneity did not allow that! So she would be herself (initially, we would sometimes be embarrassed), but still she infected those around her with her laughter. Yes, Marcia's disability influenced how we operated in some particular social setting or other, but her personality more than compensated for any differentiation in our interactions. We worked hard to enjoy ourselves as any "normal" family would and to have fun despite the differences.

What may seem strange to a family without a child with a disability is that none of this seemed unusual to us. It was just what our lives were like. We didn't know anything different. I stress this fact because others perceived our lives as not normal. But to us, it was all normal. This type of life was what we knew life to be. So, I now understand even *more* clearly how life without caregiving is not a complete life to me.

What is fascinating about a large family such as ours is the multitude of varying stories that can be told. And we did have a large family: two older brothers (Jim and Ron), me, Arlene, then the twins (Marcia and Debbie) and my parents. And each of us has our own stories to tell about growing up in our family. We can tell greatly varying stories about the same incident, each having our own perspectives and feelings about the event. One of the messages I want to share is that the siblings of a child with a disability have vastly different perspectives on their family's life than do the parents. And those perspectives led us each down different paths; it was the same journey, but we each took different forks in the road.

The following chapter is devoted to how growing up beside Marcia affected me and my siblings, how we have made adjustments in our lives because of her, and how these adjustments left me gifts that would forever change the way I thought.

***

Family Perspectives

"Marcia never complained about all her hardships, but down deep I know she would've liked to be 'normal' like her siblings."

~ Helen Wallace

Gift #1: Embrace Diversity

Someone once said that the problem with life is that it must be lived looking forward, while learning takes place looking backward. In hindsight, this is how our family lived each day, each month, and each year with Marcia. We didn't ask ourselves what we were learning from her as a person with a disability; we just did what was needed to help her, because she was our sister, and we loved her. We looked forward to having fun with her each new day. Looking back over time, I have come to know that we have learned much more from Marcia than she ever learned from us. We have been influenced by her in ways that none of us could have known or predicted as children. For me, this is perhaps one of the most important lessons I have learned from living with Marcia: that while each person in a family is shaped by the presence of a child or sibling with a disability, each one experiences them from within the boundaries of his or her own life in a way that is diverse and unpredictable. We cannot judge others and how one acts or thinks; we are all products of the sum of our experiences in life. In order to get to know someone, we must try to understand his or her past.

Our parents relied on the experiences in their faith to explain why they had been given a child with a disability, and they reconciled the situation through their belief that God gives a person born with a disability to a family that can handle it. That was God's wish, and they accepted it as His will, and, being of a certain generation, they didn't question the hand they were dealt.

My sister Debbie took a different route than the one my parents took in coming to terms with a family member with a disability. In the end, hers was a circuitous route back to faith—faith in the service of humanity. Debbie found her purpose by serving families in a non-traditional church environment, unlike anything we ever studied in the Catholic faith. Her beliefs in the faith we knew no longer existed for her, yet the route she took still revolved around helping others. For, like many in her generation, she sought extrication from the uncertainties that life presented her by striving to make the world a better place.

We were all impacted by our unique family at very young ages. Debbie says she does recall that her young playmates that came over to play at our house had different reactions to her twin. Some expressed sympathy, some expressed curiosity, some even asked if she felt *guilty* to have a sister with a disability. Early on, Debbie felt these reactions were odd, as she didn't recognize anything to feel sorry or guilty about.

I recall one Saturday afternoon when Marcia and I decided to go to the movies. I don't remember what we were going to see, but I do know that it was a comedy. The truth is that I liked to take her to comedies, since they were something I could easily share with her. And, perhaps more importantly, I could learn from her laughter how to laugh myself. I was a "serious kid" (what they might call a "geek" today), and being with Marcia gave me permission to be sillier than I would otherwise have allowed myself to be. When going to the theater, we always planned for a little extra time because we walked slowly, and it always took us a little longer than usual to get to our seats. That day, the movie had already started, so we had to be careful and walk deliberately down the darkened theater aisle, slowly placing one foot in front of the other, trying not to fall down any steps or bump into any theater seats or the people in them. The two people walking down the aisle behind us began to make crude remarks about us, because they were unable to understand why we were walking so slowly. I said nothing to them, since we were in the show and I didn't want to disturb anybody. But I won't ever forget that experience of being purposely embarrassed just because others didn't "get it." All people are different and deserve respect, and being that rude to others only reflects on the thoughtless person's own unbounded prejudice and ignorance.

When we were finally seated, I leaned over and whispered to Marcia that the people behind us were not very nice people and that she should ignore them. She shrugged as if to say it wasn't any big deal. She did ignore them, not out of cowardice, but out of respect for the other patrons in the theater. Still, I knew those inconsiderate people had made her feel bad, and this, in turn, made me feel bad, too; not only because it had happened when I was supposedly taking care of her, but because this sort of thing happened to Marcia *all the time*. While she learned early on that these sorts of things were simply part of her life that needed to be shrugged off, I was not so fortunate. And although I have, by now, gotten over feeling angry and resentful at such occurrences, it really bothered me then to see how those people who didn't know a thing about Marcia, other than that she had a disability, would have the audacity to judge and ridicule her that way. But that *was* how life was with my sister. Yes, indeed; Marcia *was* different. She was wise beyond her years. If there is one thing that I can look back and say I learned from being with Marcia at such times, it is that there is no room in anybody's life for prejudice, because each of us is different, and it is through our differences that we show each other what it is to be human.

In her notes to me, Debbie speaks endearingly of Marcia with great warmth and fondness. She recounts, for instance, a time when she and her boyfriend took Marcia to see Barry Manilow in concert. Marcia loved his music, and she could not help herself from singing along with him—out loud—while the rest of the audience was listening to the concert in hushed silence. Remember, Marcia simply did not do things *quietly*; she always seemed to make an entrance, to outwardly show her inner spirit and joy. She enjoyed life and did not see the need to hide her feelings.

Perhaps Debbie's most profound and enduring memory of Marcia came when Debbie was a few years younger. She was lying in bed early in the morning, listening to the soft "squishing" sounds Marcia made in her sleep, thinking about her life, how different she was from her twin, and how she had gotten here and where she was going. All of a sudden, she found herself hovering in the air above her bed. She describes the moment as being peaceful, exhilarating and wonderful. She credits Marcia as having been a catalyst in this extraordinary episode, which Debbie describes as being one of the beginning steps in her adventure of self-discovery.

My earlier view was that Debbie was overly connected to Marcia and had that "special connection" you hear about between twins. While there was some truth to that, after reading Debbie's story, I see that, from *her* perspective, there wasn't that "unusual twin connection." Yes, she was impacted, as when Marcia died, for example, and at that moment Debbie awoke from a sound sleep at the touch of someone. But from her point of view, she was not "connected." Like each of us, she was living within the boundaries of her own life, asking questions and forming perspectives on embracing diversity that would not come into focus for years.

That focus sharpened abruptly for Debbie when she enrolled in an overseas study program. It was a time in her life when she was actively searching for her own identity, searching, among other things, for reasons why luck had singled her out to be the twin who could achieve whatever she wanted while her sister was "locked in her body" for life because an umbilical cord had, by chance, twisted itself around Marcia's neck instead of her own.

Up to that point, Debbie's life had seemed very much like ours, but then, suddenly, she joined a totally different faith, one which was very foreign to all of the basics we had learned as children. We realized that her life really wasn't the same; outwardly it had appeared one way, but what she truly felt was something entirely different. In joining this new church, Debbie found a sympathetic belief structure to grasp hold of, which our family or our Catholic faith could not provide her.

As a spiritual roadmap delineating an alternate path leading to truth and meaning, Debbie's new faith was radically unlike the one she had followed her entire life. But, unknown to us, Debbie had begun to feel that she needed to get outside the orthodoxy of our faith in order to look at her life afresh. She found that new vantage in this faith, which helped her gain perspective and find answers to those imponderable questions of chance, inequality, and injustice that she couldn't find alone or in the Catholic faith.

At first, we did not understand why or how profoundly Debbie's whole belief system had changed. We thought it was just a phase. But she has stuck with it, and just as she has grown accustomed to not having to defend her beliefs, we have come to understand that the unique road she took was one that worked for her. Now, we talk and work together to sort through our differences in perspective, so that her membership in her selected church is no longer an issue among us. Moreover, she has found ways, through trial and error, to incorporate her new beliefs and practices into the caregiving she extends to others, including our parents, without infringing on their beliefs or compromising her own. We have found ways to understand her unique belief system. We all, after all, should expect respect from one another, no matter how different.

My younger sister Arlene is a registered nurse by trade who later became a midwife. She herself says she went into the medical profession in part because, as a child, she was a nurse to Marcia, helping her get through her seizures. As described earlier, one of Arlene's clearest memories of Marcia is when Marcia experienced her first seizure. Another of Arlene's most vivid memories of growing up with Marcia is from when Arlene was nine. She had read and reread, "at least fifty times," *Karen, by Marie Lyons Killilea*, a book about the author's daughter, who had cerebral palsy. It gave Arlene a view of her sister she had not had till then, a view that Marcia really *was* special, that Marcia was different but provided a perspective on life to us even as young children. She was in our lives for some purpose to help us form our future paths. And as she realized for the first time what it actually meant for Marcia to have a disability, it produced in her an awareness of sadness beyond her years.

Years later, when Arlene was getting married, she asked Marcia to be her bridesmaid. Arlene asserts now that she had wanted a big wedding mostly so that Marcia could take part in it. As siblings, we often tried to incorporate into our lives the pure delight we knew Marcia would find in such celebrations. Our siblings typically revel in our family weddings and love to be part of the ceremony. But for Marcia, she had come to learn not to expect to be included in "normal occurrences." So Marcia's delight at being able to march down the aisle with her sister is a memory that Arlene truly cherishes. You can see how Marcia was always foremost in our minds in life's major decisions. But she was just our sister, and there was nothing unusual about this.

My brothers, Jim and Ron, loved Marcia as dearly, and were as protective of her, as any of the girls in our family. But perhaps because they were the older siblings—Jim was nine years older and Ron six years older than Marcia—and because they were males, their life paths were a little different from the ones the girls took. As they were growing up, they sheltered Marcia within the family cocoon just as doggedly as their sisters did, and I think both were impacted by Marcia, but in a different way than the girls were. Unlike Debbie, Arlene, and me, the boys didn't naturally assume responsibility for Marcia's care the way we did. My parents, not wanting their children to be consumed by Marcia's needs, made certain that, like us, the boys did things outside the home—which is, after all, the conventional role differentiation that men and women have embarked upon traditionally. We were a traditional family in most senses of the word. Girls were supposed to grow up to be caregivers; boys were supposed to grow up to be breadwinners. Later in life, though, we did see life experiences alter the traditional roles.

This is not to say that my brothers cared any less for Marcia than we did. Nothing could be further from the truth. Their varying degrees of interaction with Marcia only point to one of the lessons I have learned over my years of working in this field: let people do what they can according to their strengths and, additionally, accept their contributions as being indicative of the best they have to offer.

Jim, the oldest, a chemist and the father of three children, is perhaps the most serious and intellectual of my siblings. I do not think he would disagree if I say he has difficulty expressing himself emotionally, in much the same way my father did. To this day, he does not easily express the emotions that a person with disabilities, such as Marcia, evokes, or those brought on by illness, such as my mother's dementia or my father's lung disease. It is just who he is, genetically and by upbringing. In other words, to ask him to assume primary caregiving responsibilities for someone like Marcia or my mother would be to ask him to do something for which he is not innately skilled. On the other hand, Jim expressed his love for Marcia more metaphorically, in that he compensated for the emotional distance he was comfortable with by spending huge amounts of time and effort around the holidays trying to find Marcia the most unique, creative, and appropriate gift available.

I recollect one particular Christmas when we were older: all the stores in Chicago were sold out of a toy that he wanted to get Marcia, but he wouldn't give up and, finally, he managed to find a store somewhere in Illinois or Wisconsin or Ohio that still had one of those toy parrots that would mimic what was said to it. Jim simply *had* to have it, because he knew how much Marcia loved auditory games and toys, and when she opened her present and the parrot repeated and repeated again something like "Wow! Look at the great parrot!" it was clear to everyone that it was indeed the perfect gift. Marcia couldn't stop laughing. Of course, whenever Marcia laughed, we all did. And, in this case, so did the parrot ... over and over and over. As Marcia laughed and her arms went up in the air with joy, Jim beamed with pleasure.

I can't remember another holiday when there was more laughter. I'm afraid we wore down that poor parrot's battery before the other presents were even opened. I don't know where or how we managed to get more batteries, given that it was Christmas, but we somehow kept that bird squawking with laughter and sidelong comments for the whole time we were there at home. So, my brother compensated symbolically for his lack of direct involvement by being the best brother he could be at Christmas.

The other way in which Jim related to Marcia was through his pranks. Those pranks were the basis of the relationship that allowed Jim to be comfortable with Marcia's disabilities. One day, he told Marcia that a squirrel had gotten into the house and that he thought it was hiding in the basement. Marcia knew instinctively that he was teasing her, but they carried on their charade for quite some time. The rules of their game were well-known and appreciated by both of them. Marcia, for instance, knew that Jim would expect her to start bossing him around in a search for the phantom squirrel, so she might intone with mock sarcasm, "Well, Jimbo, have you looked in the closet yet? If I were a squirrel, it would be the *first* place I would go and hide." And Jim would say something like, "Well, Marcia, that's because you like to hang out with the other nuts. If you were a squirrel, I think the first place I'd look for you would be inside the piano. And you know what? If I caught you hiding in there, I'd take you into the basement and hang you by the tail from the water pipes!" And Marcia would respond with something like, "But you're the one who's a drip! Not me! You're the one who should be hung from the water pipes. Do you know why?" And of course Jim would know why, but Marcia would answer for him gleefully: "So you could dry out!" Exchanges like this would, of course, produce predictable howls of laughter from each of them, and the game would persist until someone would finally say something like, "I guess the darned squirrel managed to get away again. Oh, well."

This type of playful bantering was never malicious or mean, even though both Jim and Marcia could at various times be caustic in their remarks; it was simply a method they employed to maintain the status quo between them. Today, such give-and-take interactions would probably be categorized under a clinical heading of "art therapy" or "game therapy," whereby people use proscribed techniques to confront large and troubling issues in their lives by employing their imaginations to recreate the issues in forms to which they can more easily relate and manage. In Jim and Marcia's case, as well as in my brother Ron's, they utilized humor to represent the larger issues confronting Marcia and our family. Back then, though, their reenactment of trusted and comfortable themes, such as the wayward squirrel, was how Jim, with Marcia's active participation, learned to cope with his little sister's disabilities—through play.

The other area of Jim's life that allowed Marcia to "show her stuff" was Marcia's own interest in being a caregiver. Jim and his wife, Denise, had three children. Marcia would visit their home on Friday evenings and "help babysit." While visiting, she became her bossy self, made sure all of the toys were put away, and took charge of things as she liked to do. We can all still hear her instructions to "put the toys away neatly!"

My other brother, Ron, perhaps because he was a little closer to Marcia in age, was around more often than Jim. A self-employed computer consultant now, he was once a business manager of a larger company, but through reevaluation of his life he has chosen a less complicated lifestyle. Unlike Jim, he wears his emotions closer to the surface and allows himself to be more engaged empathetically with his environment. Ron had a mischievous streak, which he took out on Marcia as a way to include her in his fun and to communicate to her that he considered her a worthy playmate. Both he and Jim played games with Marcia, for it was a tried-and-true way to cope with serious matters that defied easy explanations, such as why our sister was unable to walk.

For instance, Marcia needed help in tying her shoes, and she made it clear to people that her laces had to be fastened "just so." As anyone with children knows, whenever a parent or a sibling demands that something be done "just so," it begs for retribution, as a way to keep things on an even keel. Knowing instinctively about the fallibility of perfectionism, Ron, teaming up with his wife, Annee, would sneak up on Marcia and untie her shoes or tie them together. Marcia, of course, was in on the game, and she would glare at Ron and say, "What are you doing?" Like Ron and Jim's mischievousness, hers was brimming with mock indignation, and the entire game, which was repeated many times with endless variations, serves to show how a stigmatizing situation can be transformed, through humor, into one of acceptance, in a way that does not diminish anybody's role. It also serves to show that in families that have a member with a disability, there are many indirect ways to communicate the esteem and respect crucial to maintaining balance within the family.

Another example of how equilibrium is maintained in a unique family like ours is in how we all pitched in to help Marcia with her "patterning," which was a technique that was supposed to help bridge the gaps in the developmental steps Marcia's cerebral palsy was denying her. This meant that we would come home from school and assist Marcia in going through a variety of movements that mimicked those of the developmental stage Marcia was supposed to be traversing. So, before Ron and I and my sisters could go out and play after school, we came home and all took turns crawling around on the floor with Marcia. Or else we each took a hand or a leg while she was on a table and then, with five of us helping her, we moved her limbs through the motions of ordinary creeping and crawling and such. Unless there was something that really demanded our attention, like a surprise visit by a best friend, we rarely complained about having to do it, and we just did it. Was it "normal" for us to crawl around on the floor after school? No. But we did it to help Marcia and, because of that, it seemed absolutely normal to us.

And this point is crucial: life with Marcia was the norm, for us and for her. My parents made sure of this, because, consciously or unconsciously, they knew that anything less would have meant that we were, in effect, patronizing Marcia, and we and she, in turn, would have been diminished as humans in the eyes of God by it.

My parents became experts at trying to keep things normal for the rest of us, and at not making us feel guilty for living our own lives. Every single one of us remembers that fact. It didn't seem so extraordinary to us as children, but now, as we look back at specific instances, it is clear to us that this was a concerted effort on our parents' part, and I'm sure it was not an easy one at times. Arlene specifically told me a story about a time she had wanted to go to a lake with a friend but made the choice to not go, as she felt she should be home with Marcia. Mom encouraged her to go and, released by my mother's injunction to go have fun, she had a wonderful time, feeling no guilt. Debbie told me a similar story about coming home from school and wanting to go bike riding with her friends. She had also made the decision to stay home with Marcia, until Mom, being "so coooool" as Debbie called it, insisted that she go with her friends. She, too, specifically remembers having felt no guilt and having had a wonderful time. I myself remember many, many similar times. I guess I would have to say that Mom became an expert at letting us know it was okay to be ourselves and to not feel guilty about pursuing our own lives.

Later in life, as adults, Mom did share with me that this attempt to encourage her children to live their own lives was indeed a concentrated effort on her part, which we surely didn't know as children. In this way, our mother (and our father, too) taught us not only to accept ourselves for who we were, but also to appreciate our own uniqueness and that of others. From them, I learned very early on in life that not everyone was like me, that we were all unique, and that uniqueness itself was normal and something to be embraced.

Through this process of acceptance of myself and others, I have learned tolerance, which is perhaps the most valuable lesson a child can be taught. But, like all of life's other lessons, tolerance is complicated by other factors, some of which are contradictory. As a child, life for me was simple: I was able to select (or rather deselect) my friends based simply upon their acceptance of my sister. As an adult, things have become vastly more complicated: I cannot control what others feel or how they behave or the level of their ability to accept differences. That is, as an adult, selection of friends, lovers, and associates comes to depend on a variety of intervening and sometimes opposing factors, which are not always easy to identify, at least at first.

Time and experience have given me insight into what Marcia knew from the very beginning, and into the lessons my parents tried to teach me. It all boils down to one simple fact: it really *does* matter what people I surround myself with. I know now as never before that I need to cultivate relationships with people who truly appreciate and accept the differences in other people. I try now to seek out and surround myself with people who are tolerant. But tolerance, like life's other virtues, is learned. And it is one of Marcia's and my parents' special gifts to me. Tolerance is at the core of what I have learned from them: Let people do what they can, according to their unique strengths and to their own needs. Don't judge those who cannot, for whatever reason, give, in the same way or the same amount, of themselves as you do. Accept and celebrate uniqueness. I have used and reused this gift many times in my life. I'm sure I will continue to find ways to use it forever, for as I said earlier, the problem with life is that it must be lived looking forward, while learning takes place looking backward.

***

Gift #2: Discover Your Purpose

I was the eldest sister, and so perhaps my natural role was to step in and provide care for people. My sister Arlene teases me about this. She gave me a calendar, once, spoofing people who take on too much responsibility; each day on the calendar had something about how to quit taking responsibility and relax. That calendar gave me quite a few chuckles, but I certainly did not see myself just "taking time off" from any responsibility. The fact is, I simply took responsibility where I saw there was a need. The more responsibility the better, in my mind. For instance, there was no discussion with my parents about their aging and their fears about who was going to be there for Marcia. I volunteered for that responsibility myself, because I knew that it was important to my parents. I was the one involved in the facility where Marcia lived. In other words, I had the expertise and the ability to help where and when it was needed.

The road of life has turns in it that we don't see until we're past them—if *ever*. By gazing back through time, I see that my whole life's purpose and understanding of how each of us possesses unique and priceless gifts began with my sister. Perhaps knowingly, Marcia gave me the ability to view life in a "different way." A true gift, it is an ability that has set my life on a course that leads directly from her and allows me to gain perspective on what really matters.

I am reminded of a client I met recently who was just graduating from college. After graduation, she took a trip and was bitten by a mosquito and contracted encephalitis. Following that, she experienced hundreds of seizures a year, often having seizures during our meetings.

That person looked at me during one of our interviews and said, "You understand what I'm talking about when I'm talking to you. You can understand me." I went home from that interview thinking, *My personal life could be crumbling, but it would be nothing. I could fix it.* It reaffirmed my conviction that my ability to see others' needs and provide caregiving solutions was exactly what I was supposed to be doing with my life. It was *my* purpose.

As she was growing up, Arlene, like the rest of us, did her part in taking care of Marcia's needs, such as helping her to get dressed and assisting her to stand. Those duties were simply part of our job to "play nurse" with our sister. It wasn't a burden any more than it was a burden helping Mom keep the house clean. It was play. We loved Marcia; we loved playing with her.

But for some people, their play activities as children mirror more than they may realize until much later, when their inner passion moves them in a particular direction. This is the case with my sister Arlene, whose whole career path was unconsciously defined for her when she was in grade school. She instinctively knew her purpose, even as a child. Arlene admitted to me recently that only now does she realize the full impact that "playing nurse" had on her life.

Our mother had told us many times that she could not imagine Marcia living without her. Her purpose was to make sure Marcia had the fullest and safest life possible. But she also always said that she hoped Marcia would not outlive her. As a young adult, it was difficult for Arlene to understand that. Now, as a mother herself, Arlene says that she has a much better understanding of our mother's wish. The need to protect our children, especially ones that might depend on others for their lifetime care, is an overwhelming purpose and responsibility. It is both an obligation and a privilege, and it is one that we want to keep for ourselves and not pass on to another.

You will recall I have mentioned that my brothers had a difficult time participating in the writing of this book. Sometimes, we take on a responsibility that is overwhelming, but the instinctive purpose that is within us drives us to go beyond what we might normally be capable of doing. For example, Ron and his wife Annee had, for several years, taken on the responsibility of being weekend caregivers for my parents, driving six hours every week to relieve me and the other caregivers for the weekend. His two children had recently graduated from college, and they were searching for their own independence. Ron was feeling so emotionally drained from that and from my father's subsequent death that he found he had less emotional currency to spend at that moment. This overextension of responsibility, in itself, points to a lesson that all caregivers learn eventually, usually the hard way: your resources, despite what you believe and wish of yourself, are finite. My other brother Jim has had his own personal tragedy in the untimely death of his son, Stephen. This restricted his ability to emotionally participate in the writing of this book. We, as a family, have learned that if you go to the emotional well over and over and over again without replenishing it, it dries up, and you experience empathy fatigue. Sometimes, just as in the world of aquifers, when a well goes dry, the bearing strata can become so hard and brittle that it turns impermeable, making it hard to get the water flowing again. We become hardened to the pain and suffering of others.

It is important to combat this natural overextension of ourselves, by taking the time for personal renewal and rejuvenation. But when it came to Marcia, for us the well never seemed to go dry. In fact, with Marcia, the opposite is probably truer; she was the one who replenished us, particularly with her humor, when the well ran low in our family. It wasn't a job anybody ever gave her, it was just one of the "duties" that she knew was hers. She was a natural at it. If you felt bad about anything, you needed only to visit with and talk to Marcia. It was part of *her* purpose.

The difference between my role as caregiver and that of my siblings parallels the paths we took as children. It was only natural that I, being the oldest of the three sisters, would take on the responsibility to provide care to the family as my obligation. My sisters often deferred to me in this regard and would step in and out, taking responsibility for things when it was needed, as they do today. But I have learned how to call upon my siblings when my well is about to go dry.

As for the lessons that I myself have learned from Marcia and the dynamics in my own family that revolved around her disability, perhaps the most useful gift I have received from her is how to search my soul in order to locate my own purpose. In doing so, I have discovered that my purpose is to channel my expertise and natural abilities to become an effective caregiver. I know this is true, because it brings me joy akin to the same joy Marcia's laughter brought to my family throughout her life.

***

Gift #3: Treasure the Truth

One of the most wonderful gifts Marcia bestowed upon me was the understanding of the importance of being honest and saying what was on my mind. She knew of no other way to be. There were many examples of this, and most of them were quite clear to all who were recipients of "the truth."

I remember an instance of this when I was sixteen. I was going on my first date and was a nervous wreck. I was sitting in the family living room—fidgeting with my hair—along with my father and Marcia, who were there ready to "inspect" my date. I was nervous not only because I was going out on my first date, but because I was also going to a "fancy" restaurant. Both of these were things I had never done before, since our family did not go out to eat, let alone to fancy restaurants. Would I know how to act? What if I had to go the bathroom and didn't know where it was? What if I spilled something? What if I looked fat? As if those terrors weren't enough, my father hovered over me, his oldest daughter, as it was *his* "first date," too.

The doorbell rang. I let Bob in and made the introductions. (You see, I even remember my date's name after all these years, as this day was one I was not to forget!) My father didn't ask too many questions, which was a relief. But Marcia wasn't quite so diplomatic. She wanted facts! She wanted honesty! So, the first question out of her mouth to poor Bob was, "Are you going to marry my sister?"

I wanted to crawl into a hole. Of course, as a teenager, I was by nature mortified at any suggestion, especially in front of my parents, that I might be involved in romantic commerce of any sort, or if it was potentially serious, at the prospect that my sister would put my boyfriend on the spot and scare him off. But the truth was that if any of our boyfriends couldn't handle Marcia's honesty, then we couldn't handle them.

I remember another example that happened a few years later, when I had saved enough money to purchase my first new car. Proud of my car, I wanted to show it off, so I drove to my parents' home. (I was living in my own apartment by this time.) I had owned other cars before this one, but this car was a spanking-new, beautiful white Camaro, and I was proud of myself for having been able to save enough money to buy it. I was also being extra careful to take good care of it. Everyone was home except my father, so I parked in the driveway and went into the downstairs family room to listen to the stereo and to await my father's arrival. When he finally came home, I heard a little commotion upstairs and, when nobody came down to the family room, I decided to go find out for myself what was happening. Little did I know, as I made my way to the top of the stairs, that my father had accidentally scratched my new car with his car door when he had gotten out. Hesitant to tell me, he had asked everyone to keep it quiet, because he wanted to break the news to me himself. The minute I walked into the room, however, Marcia beat him to the punch and blurted out, "Dad smashed up your car!"

Marcia never *could* keep a secret. You always knew exactly where you stood with her. I was devastated over the nick in the car's paint job, but I got over it quickly. At least my Dad was spared the confession—but not before Marcia had delivered a tongue-lashing. To this day, my friends say I'm the one among them who can be relied upon to tell things just the way they are. For this, I have Marcia to thank. She taught me that being honest and up-front were the *only* ways to be.

Arlene has learned the same thing, because in her notes to me, she was very honest. She felt she had never really grieved for Marcia. The week after Marcia passed away, she had learned that the adoption of their son was being contested and five agonizing weeks later, they had to return him to his birthparents. She and her husband then adopted a daughter a month after Marcia's death and she felt this was a sign from Marcia. But they soon discovered their new daughter had heart disease and she died 6 months later. So through all of this, Arlene confesses to having experienced "a conflicted element of relief" in her period of grieving after Marcia died. She knew our parents were getting older and they wouldn't be able to care for Marcia. Marcia was so close to our parents. How would she handle their deaths? How would we care for into the future? So, in a sense, Arlene felt caught in a bind by Marcia's disability, and when Marcia died, Arlene experienced a complex and conflicting range of emotions that included among them a lifting of the pressure brought on by responsibility.

This admission by Arlene points to another lesson I think she has learned from Marcia, as well as from heartbreaking tragedies in her own life: that in order to perform the duties required of her in her life and in her job, she needs to determine the scope of the responsibilities she assumes, or she invites the danger of becoming too involved in and too hurt by them. This lesson in the usefulness and limits of empathy comes, I think, directly from her experiences with Marcia and in having come to know the fragility and heartache of life firsthand. Another lesson that Arlene's candidness about her feelings point to is that the emotions that swirl through many of the events in a family with a person who has disabilities *are* complex and frequently conflicting, and only time, forgiveness, reflection, and, above all, honesty can begin to unsnarl all of the nuances.

After Marcia's death, Arlene went on to adopt four children, and she has become a great mother in her own right. But because, like Marcia, it is in her character that things need to be "just so," she struggles, as she did when she was younger, with finding the right mix between obligation and selflessness in her effort to be as good a mother as she can be for her children. In having had Marcia as her sister, Arlene knows she has gained an irreplaceable perspective on this ongoing struggle to define the extent and limits of her caregiving, which she would not have had otherwise. In other words, Marcia's lessons in the usefulness and limits of empathy have helped Arlene to be honest with *herself*. This, in turn, has allowed her to be authentic with others. This is a gift that she will always carry with her, for in the end it is a way for her to know her own soul as she shares herself with others.

This gift has set a baseline for my life. I find that when I am unsure as to what direction to take, the truth seems to clear the path for me. I am able to be honest not only with others, but also with myself. As they say, "the truth shall set you free."

***

Family Obligations & Hard Decisions

"There were many health problems, but Marcia always coped well with them. The year before she died, Marcia became much more independent. If she could do a task, she really did not want help."

~ Helen Wallace

Gift #4: Acknowledge and Learn from Diversity

I was a typical teenage girl and probably not an easy child to raise, as I was way too independent and always on the go. I was a baton twirler and competed out of town on the weekends. I was bright in high school, and I had many friends. However, I was always very conscious through the high school years to involve Marcia in activities. My boyfriends *had* to like Marcia. If they didn't like her and didn't treat her well, they were not my boyfriends. If my other friends didn't accept her, they weren't my friends, either. But my friends did accept her. In our community, there were only a few rare occasions when people would stare at her like she was some sort of sideshow curiosity.

I can remember one particular time that Marcia and I went into a supermarket, where we realized that a woman was following us around, up and down the aisles, as if she was just shopping. But we soon realized she wasn't really buying anything but instead staring at Marcia, who was holding on to our shopping cart for support as she walked. I don't know if the woman was just curious or repelled, or maybe both and morbidly curious. In any case, I finally grew fed up with her ogling, which was not at all subtle, and turned to her. "You know," I said, "you don't know how lucky you are that you have two good legs." The woman blushed and hurried off, embarrassed that she had been caught. After she was gone, Marcia turned to me and said gleefully, "That's giving it to 'em, Mary Anne!"

Marcia continued to have an impact on my life, through my teen years into young adulthood. But the presence of Marcia and the undeniable pull that home exerted on me could not prevent me from wanting to venture forth out into the world. My first stop would be college. The day finally came when all the preparations had been made and papers signed and dormitories assigned, and I went away to college. But all the best-laid plans could not alter the fact that, no sooner had I gotten there, I began to grow homesick. I mean *really* homesick. Was it my friends I missed? Was it my family? Was it my boyfriend? I think the truth is that it was probably a combination of all those things.

But it didn't matter. All that really mattered to me was that the pull back home was momentous, and I couldn't resist it. Finally, unable to bear being away, I called my father in tears. "I can't stay here. I hate it. Come and get me," I cried. So he came and took me home before the first semester was even over.

After that episode, I enrolled in a local junior college for two years and, during that time, lived at home, because that's where I was most comfortable. Was I at home one hundred percent of the time? No. I was eighteen. At that age the world revolved around me. But somewhere in the back of my mind, I knew it was out of character for me, who was so independent, to also be so homesick.

A few months after I came home, I had what I call my "Ah Ha!" moment, in which I became consciously aware not only of why I had been so homesick, but also of what was really important to me.

Everybody has these sorts of revelatory moments when events that may have moved you subconsciously one way or another along your life path rise to consciousness in one sudden flash of insight. My moment came when I was twenty, going to school at night and working, and I suddenly realized one day that the largest part of who I was revolved around enjoying being a caregiver. I can't remember the exact moment, and there were no bugles or drumbeats announcing it, but the message to me was loud and clear. I had thought that maybe I had left college due to missing a boyfriend, but after coming home from college and then later breaking up with him, I still felt the same tug toward home. The truth was that I had missed being around Marcia and caring for her. Being one of Marcia's caregivers gave my life meaning in a way that school hadn't or, as I would learn eventually, a career couldn't unless it was catalyzed, at its core, with providing care to people.

This revelation took the shape of me realizing that I had a responsibility not only to Marcia, but also to my parents. I still had too many oats to sow to assume all the responsibility for Marcia's care, but nonetheless, I did have a profound sense at that moment of being unable to leave them with all the responsibility. Basically, I saw that it just wasn't fair to them. After all, my parents had devoted themselves for over twenty years to our family's well-being and, in particular, to seeing to it that their most vulnerable child received the best care and most protection they could provide. They had worked diligently to provide for us and had forsaken vacations and other frills that, I thought, were their due. So, I knew that if I didn't step in before too long, they would continue caring for her in the same manner, and they would be denied, until who knows when, the opportunity to have a life of their own.

Being a "type A" sort of person, I wanted to connect with the world in a proactive way, so eventually I moved out from my parents' home. I took an apartment in Mt. Prospect, the next town over from Des Plaines. I was twenty-one. I had made my decision; my life course would be directed in such a way that home would always be the central point from which I ventured. For instance, I was often at my parents' home on Sunday for dinner, and I later helped Marcia at Clearbrook at various times during the week, where she was attending day programs geared to individuals with disabilities. Mostly, I was "just around," helping out wherever I could. Because I was always there, my brother Jim teased me that he really didn't think I had an apartment somewhere else.

In my midtwenties, I entered a period in which home was moved away for me by a career that took me traveling for several financial institutions. In fact, I was a workaholic. By the time I was twenty-one, I had a full-time job as a computer programmer, I took a full load of classes at school, and I worked as a bartender at night. I did this for two years until I finished my schooling. In all of this, there wasn't a lot of extra time. What time there *was* I tried to spend partying with my friends, going skiing in Colorado, and such things. In hindsight, though, I always brought Marcia back to my life, even when I was in those "selfish" years.

One episode, during this period, that illustrates my constant attraction to home and to Marcia came in 1975, when I was twenty-five and Marcia was turning twenty-one. This story relates my wish to give Marcia as many experiences in life as I had, sometimes to my parents' dismay.

I shared my apartment with a couple of young women. We did some of the wild things men and women do at that age. When Marcia's twenty-first birthday came around, I wanted to throw her a birthday party in my apartment. After all, my friends had done the same for me, so I wanted to pass the torch along to Marcia. I suppose it was a typical party for that period; my friends were young and brash and upwardly mobile, urban professionals like me. I picked up Marcia from my parents' home and brought her to my apartment. During our typical struggle up the stairs of my old three-flat apartment, Marcia gave me her regular lecture as to why did I have to live on the third floor when I knew she would be visiting often. Once we got up to the apartment and were all settled in, she, of course, gave me the second lecture as to why didn't I just live at home; I could save money and be with her, and Mom and Dad wouldn't worry about me. I wouldn't have to have that old couch with the spring that was sticking out—and so on. (Maybe that is where I got to be such a worrier, too: from her!)

The party finally got started, and we had a great time. My friends were Marcia's friends; they, too, wanted this day to be special. There was wine and smart talk, and Marcia seemed to be thoroughly enjoying herself. There were games and music and just plain fun. I guess I wasn't paying close enough attention, though, because when things began to wind down, I discovered that Marcia had been gulping down her wine like she gulped her milk and had quietly gotten herself drunk. Completely soused! Blotto! Of course, this was, in a sense, irresponsible behavior on my part; I was the older sister who should know better. The alcohol could have reacted adversely with her seizure medications and given her a seizure. She could have fallen and hurt herself. Shame on me!

Before I could flail myself too much about giving Marcia an experience of which I knew my parents would definitely disapprove, Marcia turned to me and, in a drunken tone, shared with me how much she had loved the party. The truth is, she and I were of the age, despite her disabilities, that we got into trouble on principle alone. Frankly, I wanted her to get into trouble with me in a situation that would be relatively safe. Did we think ahead to what the consequences might have been in getting Marcia drunk? Of course not. Was I irresponsible? A little. Was it fun? Yes! Emphatically, and I would do it again! Now, saying that, Marcia never wanted wine again, and my parents didn't talk to me for two months!

This last was the sentiment that turned out to be the most lasting one for Marcia about that evening of revelry. She had fun in spite of whatever prohibitions she or we may have violated. She would use the occasion as ammunition to tease me every time after that when she would introduce me to a friend or teacher or counselor. Assuming the tone of mock indignation that she used so effectively, she would announce, "This is the sister who got me drunk when I was twenty-one," as she laughed her infectious laugh. But there was no disguising the pride she felt just in being able to make such an accusation.

Today, more than anything else, this sense of accomplishment, backhanded as it may seem, and the obvious pride Marcia felt in having partaken in something that was as "normal" as getting drunk with friends illustrates, to me, how much value Marcia attached to being included in all her family's activities, despite her limitations.

***

Gift #5: Value the Importance of Independence

Looking back, it's clear now that none of these life-altering things that happened to me occurred dramatically all at once. Life isn't generally like that. We make day-to-day decisions and muddle through things and gradually arrive at a vantage in our lives where we can say that, yes, indeed, things have changed. But that is not to say that hard decisions were not involved along the way with some of these changes in our family, because they were. I was, myself, party to two of these difficult decisions. One began when I was thirty-eight. I had just reached the realization that I wanted to step in to help my parents with Marcia, no matter what the cost to my own independence. The other tough decision was my parents' to make, and I could only watch as they aged ten years in the space of a week, making the decision to move Marcia into Clearbrook's residential facility.

My difficult decision was not so much a single one but a series of interlocking choices pertaining to how much and how quickly I should insert myself into the role of Marcia's caregiver without invalidating my parents' role. In other words, I didn't want to appear to be shoving them aside just because they were getting old and I was the "expert," since, by then, I had begun my career as a financial advocate, specializing in planning for individuals with disabilities. It was clear that they could use, and would appreciate, the help I could offer.

My parents' difficult decision came when Marcia had just turned thirty-four. Over the years, she had been enrolled in a workshop at Clearbrook, where her job was to crush aluminum cans, which, given her disability, was a task she could accomplish reasonably well and one in which she took pride. Over the years, openings would only periodically become available in Clearbrook's ninety-bed residential facility, the Commons, because of its popularity and the demand for such accommodations. There had been a ten-year waiting list. My parents always dismissed invitations to move Marcia there as being unwarranted, since they wanted to keep Marcia with them, where, in their minds, she would unquestionably receive the best care. After all, there's no place like home! But Marcia was now an adult, and, as such, her views had to be taken into serious consideration when making any such decisions concerning the future course of her life.

I must have been at a point in my own life and career where I felt confident enough about my own abilities and my own caregiving responsibilities that I could see with equanimity that both sides of this equation were now at last equally valid. It was time to question the decision to keep Marcia at home, without being unfair or favoring either alternative.

I can remember the conversation that took place that day as if it had happened yesterday. It was late in the afternoon and we were in my parents' living room where, as a child, for five years I had crawled on the floor with Marcia after school, trying to get her arms and legs to work like mine. Marcia wasn't back from the workshop at Clearbrook yet. My father had received a call from Clearbrook, notifying him that there was a residential opening for which Marcia was eligible. When I asked my father what he wanted to do about the Commons, he said, as usual, "We're not ready for Marcia to move away." I said, "But, Dad, what about Marcia? She might be ready." To his credit, my Dad saw the truth in this immediately, and when Marcia came home, I went to her to have a discussion about the possibility of moving to Clearbrook. Marcia and I talked about how the rest of us had moved out to our own apartments and maybe it was her turn to consider some independence, as well. "So, what do you want to do?" I asked. Marcia's reply, as always, was to the point. "Everybody else has moved out. So, I think I want to do that, too." But then, keenly aware of the two-way needs in their relationship, she added, "But what will Mom and Dad do if I move out? What would they do without me?"

This response was not at all unusual for Marcia, whose sensitivity and consideration to the needs of others had always been acute; she really was worried about what my parents would do without her. She knew and appreciated that they had devoted themselves to her. But Marcia, I think, also recognized that sometimes the more difficult road is the right one. Now, this is not to say that Marcia really wanted to move away from my parents. She was totally connected to them, and it was hard for anyone to imagine them not together. Indeed, Marcia's worries about my parents were not unfounded, for our mother and father figuratively tortured themselves for a week in grappling with this decision. The only comparison I can make to how weighty and difficult the decision was for them was not fully appreciated by me at the time. Not until only recently did I understand the anguish my parents went through, when I myself had to make the choice to move my mother into a nursing facility; "torture" describes the decision-making process I went through, unequivocally. For my parents, whom I watched become older in the space of a week, it must have been ten times harder. But in the end, they decided it was time for Marcia to move out. I'm not sure that it was a decision that they ever fully accepted as the right one. Moreover, they had none of the support systems that are now taken for granted to help them come to terms with their decision. For their generation, it seems, such matters were lonely, soul-searching ordeals with very few lights, other than their own, to guide them. But they made their decision, and they were prepared to live with it.

The move into Clearbrook was an emotional one for everyone. The entire family got involved, helping to decorate Marcia's room, finding her special things for her walls, and finding ways to make the transition go smoothly. We had a big party for her the day of the big move. Everything was purchased, decorated, and coordinated. But it was not home.

When Marcia finally did move out of our house into Clearbrook, little annoying things happened there that would not have occurred at home, simply because, from our perspective, there was not enough staff. At home, Marcia had the complete and enduring attention of two people who loved her, who would give their lives for her. At Clearbrook, she and eighty-nine others had the attention of no more than a handful of people. Most of the staff were conscientious caregivers. However, the fact of the matter was that there was no way Marcia could receive the comprehensive level of services at Clearbrook that she did at home.

Luckily, Marcia was able to express her dissatisfaction with things that occurred, and my parents were able to address them. But it wasn't as though my parents had dumped Marcia into some impersonal facility out of state and had washed their hands of her and walked away. No, the truth is they were always there, working at bingo, going to the pool with Marcia during the week, paying visits. On weekends, Marcia came home. Of course, Sunday became a day of torture for my mother and father, as the time drew near for them to take Marcia back to Clearbrook. In the end, though, I'm certain they saw that it had been the right thing for them to do, for the bonds may have been stretched, but they were never broken—and, some might say, they had even grown stronger, as they had for me.

From this experience, through which Marcia gained her independence, our family gained invaluable insights. Primary among them was the role that dignity plays in shaping the child into the adult. To quote the great American writer James Thurber, our family learned what all families, particularly those that are blessed with a child with a disabling condition, learn: dignity is "attained only when the heart and mind are lifted, equally at once, by the creative union of perception and grace." For it was through the creative union of the strength my parents gained from their faith, combined with their perception that no matter how difficult the experience was for them personally, it was the right one for Marcia, that our hearts and minds were lifted. As proof of this, we needed only to experience the expression on Marcia's face after she became independent to know that dignity is itself reflected as grace on the face of the soul.

***

Legacy of Marcia

"I know Marcia is at peace with the Lord, but somehow I still worry about her."

~ Helen Wallace

Gift # 6: Cherish Each and Every Day

This now brings me back to the funeral.

I will never forget the day Marcia died. I can actually recollect the exact moment of "the call." I had been with her the day before, at Clearbrook, on a Friday. Actually, I was working on a story about Marcia and was there to talk with her about it.

I was sitting in my office on the following morning, catching up on paperwork. I can recall exactly what I was doing, exactly what client papers were sitting on my desk in front of me. The phone rang. As I picked up the phone, expecting a client on the other end, I heard my father, but I hardly recognized his voice. "Marcia's gone …" were his words. "You need to come." Without knowing any of the details, I took in enough to know that she had had a seizure during the night, and because she couldn't turn over, she had suffocated. I had just seen her the day before. How could she be gone?

I drove as quickly as I could to the hospital where she had been taken. My parents were sitting in the waiting room, looking to me for a miracle. I could see the look they had, as I walked into the room, hoping I would take away their pain. Their despair was something I cannot begin to describe. The emptiness in my mother's eyes and the sadness in my father's voice were embedded in my brain forever that day. The loss was too great. Their Marcia was gone. They had just lost *their* purpose. It was an experience I cannot erase from my mind. The sadness and the loss were so great. I wanted to comfort them, but I could hardly deal with my own emotions at that moment. I was asked if we wanted to see my sister, and I didn't think my parents could handle it at that moment, but they gathered all of their strength to walk into the room where Marcia lay. It, too, was a scene I will never forget. To have the life, the laughter, and the spirit gone from the body in front of me was impossible. How could this be? She was with me, full of life, the day before. Did I tell her I loved her then? Did I remember to kiss her goodbye when I left? Did she know she had changed my life? Did I tell her she was my teacher? Did I tell her she inspired me? I'm sure similar thoughts were passing through my parents' minds at the same moment.

For all of us, a light in our lives had been extinguished. But in those dark moments following Marcia's death, when it seemed nothing could or would console us for our loss, the seeds of consolation had already begun to emerge, ever so slowly, in our knowledge that Marcia had lived independently for almost a decade at Clearbrook. We came to realize gradually that this accomplishment, among others, had been critical in bringing the singular radiance of self-esteem into Marcia's life. This was something none of us could have given her, because although self-esteem needs to be nurtured in order to flourish, it can be grown only from within. We saw that her success at living on her own was *her* way of measuring *her* success as a human being. Finally, we came to see that, in a sense, giving Marcia the chance to live her own life had been our greatest gift to her, for it gave *her* the chance she needed to succeed or fail. "The dignity of risk" is how I have heard some refer to this necessary, but often overlooked, component in the growth of self-esteem, by which parents and caregivers grant their children or clients the respect they need to make mistakes *on their own*. But how are any of us to learn what it is to be human, if not by living life on our own terms? That is all that Marcia asked for. It is on those terms that she lived and died, and it is on those terms that she taught me what it means to be human.

In trying, now, to measure her legacy from a vantage point more than fifteen years removed, I would have to say that the most enduring gift Marcia gave me was not any particular aspect of herself, but *her*— her entire incomparable being. My sister. My friend. My teacher. Thus the "Ah Ha" phase of my journey truly began.

In trying to convey to the reader what it's like and what it means to have a person with a disability in a family, I can only say that there are choices involved, all along the way, that must be made, and none of them are easy. Sometimes, a person with disabilities born into a family can seem like an affliction visited upon them. Other times, he or she can be seen as a blessing. Most often, I suspect, there are varying degrees of each of these views, as the family comes to terms with the reality that they will have to make innumerable decisions for this person for the rest of his or her life. In my work, I always tell parents of children with disabilities that I recognize that they hope that they live longer than that child, which is, of course, a reversal of the "usual" order. My telling them this is not an effort to be morbid on my part; it simply illustrates a fact: the length of the commitment is lifelong, and the depths of emotion it plumbs are profound.

Clearly, our family, for whatever reasons, chose to experience Marcia as a blessing. In the end, we felt fortunate that we had received the opportunity to experience an element of Grace through her. Yes, there were times, such as when we were positioned in a star pattern around Marcia moving her arms and legs, that it seemed to be more work than anybody could reasonably be asked to muster day in and day out. But those times of doubt were trivial compared to the other times, when she could make our sides split with laughter or when she would say something so honest and succinct it would take our breaths away.

Recognizing the gifts from Marcia was a process. Everybody has unique abilities, and if we look for them, we will not only find them but gain strength from them. That is how it was with Marcia; she had abilities far beyond what many of us recognized, and her impact on those around her was, and will continue to be, far greater than mine, or my parents', or any of my siblings'. In short, Marcia made us examine our own lives from a truly unique vantage, one that forces me to ask myself, every day, "What impact have I made, positively, in my life and in the lives of those around me?" In this question, I find strength. Most clearly of all, I find Marcia's laughter.

To their credit, my parents made much of this possible. Their undying dedication to Marcia, their willingness to try just about any treatment they thought held out promise to help her, and their ability to create a family in which everyone felt worthy and accepted made it possible for Marcia and our family to flourish when we could have floundered.

The lessons my parents learned were never stated explicitly. My father was the type of man who bore his responsibilities with grace and dignity—alone. In today's world, where people talk about their problems anywhere and everywhere, it seems impossible that he could have held his thoughts to himself for a lifetime. But my father did not deign it was time to convey his closely held thoughts until the night before he died, when he honored me with them. These, it happened, were his feelings on how he felt about my taking on the caregiving role for so many in my life, including my five stepchildren, Marcia, my mother, and, of course, my dad. He maintained his sense of "giving" right up until the moment he died. Although every breath he took at that time of his life was difficult, on the day before he died, he used some of those last breaths to remind me of another day in my life. He recalled to mind the day when I called home from my first semester in college, crying, homesick, and wanting to come home. He had instructed me, as I cried to him, that I didn't need to go to college; he said I should just find a nice man, get married, and have a family that I could care for. Long before I knew it myself, he saw that my mission in life was to care for others. I remember that discussion with him like it was yesterday. My life was not blessed with my own biological children. However, I do have many wonderful stepchildren that were brought into my life. My dad shared with me, on that last day of his life, that he thought I had done a wonderful job caring for my sister, my stepchildren, and my mother. He went on to say that now he was "absolving" me from the caregiving role, and that he wished for me to find someone to take care of me—*except* that I should first finish the job of caring for my mother.

As for my mother, she left me several letters, excerpts of which are included in this book, which I found after she developed dementia. After Marcia died, my mother struggled every day. With the death of my sister, she had lost her purpose. Her thoughts were consumed with what-ifs. She would see my sister in her sleep, she would think of her in her waking moments. I thought that if she could write down her thoughts about Marcia, it would help. I found her thoughts written in letters to me only years later, when I chanced to come across them folded underneath some clothes in her dresser. In both instances, my parents spoke of the concerns they had for Marcia's well-being after they were gone.

I'm certain they had waited so long to even touch on this subject because they themselves had been consumed with the responsibility for Marcia's care and did not want to burden their other children with their concerns. I would not have known the weight of that burden had I not witnessed firsthand my mother and father wrestling with the decision to move Marcia away from home into Clearbrook. Such was the depth of their anguish that in the space of one week, I saw my parents age ten years. But seeing them grow old before my eyes did not affect me as profoundly as when I myself recently had to wrestle with a decision of whether or not to find a nursing home for my mother. As I mentioned earlier, the pain and doubt and guilt were excruciating, and it is not a burden I would ever want my own children to have to carry.

So, were my parents correct in not sharing their burdens with their children? Can we truly learn from others the anguish they feel if we have not experienced it ourselves? What lessons can parents of children with disabilities share with others about the hard decisions? In answer, I can say only that the most difficult lessons cannot be shared, only experienced, and that we need each other's help to gain an appreciation of those lessons for the gifts they are. In the end, though, it is probably wisest to keep in mind the thoughts that Thurber wrote about the nature of dignity:" that it is attained only when the heart and mind are lifted, equally at once, by the creative union of perception and grace. Because, just as dignity is attained, so, too, are the lessons that are learned best shared with others, in the spirit of grace and perception". The wisdom in these words is evident. But, as I will describe in the two sections that follow, the limits of putting such wisdom into practice proved to be a very difficult and painful process for me.

***

Caregiving as a Stepmother
The Gifts Applied to Real Life

I want to diverge from my recollections of Marcia and my parents in order to share with you some of the personal insights I have gained through another form of caregiving, becoming a stepmother. My hope is that by sharing them and the lessons I have learned, I can illustrate how I applied the lessons I learned from Marcia to my own situation. By doing so, I hope also to ease others throughout difficult decision-making processes and transitions of their own, for it is my own experience that such processes and transitions often blindside us and propel us headlong, unaware, into unfamiliar territory before we are finally able to realize where we are, get our bearings, and know what is happening to us.

First, let me say that by now, I have learned that there are many valid variations of giving care. To name a few, there are parenting, brothering and sistering, and extended-familying; there is religious caregiving, and there is professional caregiving. I am certain that there are many, many other forms by which people extend care, some more valid than others but all striving for the same thing: to assist others in doing what they cannot do for themselves. I include this specific chapter on stepmothering because I have found that the gifts Marcia taught me applied to this chapter of my life far more aptly than I would have expected. Some of us are programmed to caregive, and thus we believe that we know what we are doing. But we must be careful as it then too easy to become a caregiver for anyone who needs it. We are apt to be taken advantage of. We find it easy to define ourselves in that role alone and we are then stuck in a rut. As a matter of fact, if Marcia had not left me the gifts about which I have already written, I honestly do not know how I could have made it through a period of my life that required extensive caregiving. To say I was blindsided by the experience is an understatement. To say I was overwhelmed would be closer to the truth. But neither of these interpretations can even begin to describe the toll exacted on me.

It so happened that I became a full-time stepmother of three little boys, all in a rush, when I married a man who had three children, ages one, three, and five. Through a series of events over the first year of our marriage, they came to live with us full-time.

Oh, my gosh! Was I ever unprepared! Now, let me tell you: I thought I could do this. I really did. I just needed to be loving, open, honest, and steadfast in my beliefs, right?

True, I knew how to care for others and, indeed, had made it my profession to help people extend various aspects of care to others. But most of my direct caregiving experiences had come through looking after members of my own immediate family. Moreover, I had grown into that particular job over a period extending into decades. But this situation was *different. Very, very different.* This was a ready-made family. It needed *instant* caregiving. It needed it *now.* It needed it *constantly* and *continuously.*

The boys were delightful, even though they had had a rocky start in life and were not about to accept a new stepmother, especially the oldest boy, who had trouble adjusting more than his brothers due to "time put in" with his biological mother. Like all young children, they needed time, patience, and love—a total commitment. The boys needed me to make them a home in which they felt secure and loved, but I also had a full-time career that drew my attention away from home and the boys. My struggle was one that has, by now, become a common one in families in which both parents work: how was I to balance being a mother, a wife, and a provider and honor my commitment to give each one of them the best of myself?

Over the course of the next fifteen years, I learned, the hard way, that I needed to go back to the basics that Marcia had taught me, for the opposing pressures of the struggles I encountered threatened at times to overwhelm me far beyond my wildest imagination. I had to keep reminding myself of the things I had learned from my experience of caring for Marcia, things such as "I must embrace differences," "I must be honest with my family and with myself," and "I must not only love my boys but also *show* them that I do." I recommend to any new stepmother (or stepfather) to learn these three lessons by heart. Post them on the wall if you need to. Tattoo them on the door of your waking mind. Under no circumstances make the mistake (that many primary caregivers do) of thinking that you can do everything by yourself. That is a mirage. The reality is that you can do only as much as you can. Of course, these three basic lessons are self-evident nostrums that any seasoned caregiver can easily espouse from afar. When I was in the thick of it, trying to keep everything going smoothly, while I was still building my business and trying to be a good wife, I found it seductively easy to lose sight of what was right in front of me. After all, I was a successful woman. Why couldn't I just apply myself a little more diligently here and there, plan a little more carefully, organize a little more tightly, and do it all? Indeed, this is what I tried to do. But, as a famous football coach once said about the importance of knowing your limits, "fatigue makes cowards of us all." In my efforts to be all things to all people all the time, I became blind to my own limits and, most importantly, blind to my own history. I forgot to apply the lessons Marcia had taught me, particularly the one about discovering your own purpose. I neglected the first lesson that any caregiver worth her salt knows: take care of yourself first, so that you can take care of others. As a consequence, I overextended myself. I could not see the forest for the trees, as the saying goes. If I look back and am totally honest with myself, I actually lost *me*.

Don't get me wrong—those fifteen years were some of the best years of my life, and I treasure every moment. But, honestly, it was also a period of time when it was difficult for me to maintain a sense of self, because stepparenting demanded a different set of caregiving responsibilities than the ones I was acquainted with, and, in truth, I had a great deal of trouble in the transference from one situation to another. For instance, as a stepparent, I found that I had to walk a *very* fine line between being a friend to my sons and being their caregiver. I felt myself being constantly tugged one way or the other by opposing emotional forces that I did not fully appreciate. I felt I was ceaselessly being judged by many (and by myself), mostly in the harshest manner. Consequently, I found myself second-guessing everything I did. In the middle of it all, I lost perspective on who I was. I found it hard to trust my instincts or to follow the lessons I had learned on the need to take care of myself.

For example, the boys were dependent, but they were also growing to be independent day by day. They had divided allegiances to begin with; the oldest boys were really not sure what my intentions were from the outset. There was a fragile balance in providing love and not stepping on other relationships, such as those with their father, their grandparents, and their birth mother. In a word, it was an all-consuming job. The only way I survived and prospered was to finally trust my instincts, follow the lessons I had learned from Marcia, and still take care of my own needs.

One of the things I discovered first was that stepparenting has a different reward system than the one I experienced when I provided care for my sister. The difference between the two is that, as a sister, I was not required to be "constantly on," while as a stepparent, it was the opposite: I *was* "constantly on." There were *always* feelings that needed to be soothed, cuts that needed to be tended to, appointments that needed to be kept, fights that needed to be mediated. It took me a long time to find my bearings in this new role, but once I found them and was able to define the limits of my caregiving, I became a better stepmother. Getting my footing on solid ground as a stepmother was *only* just a matter of applying the lesson I had learned from Marcia to do the best I could. I say "only" with a large dose of glibness, of course, for, in truth, it took me a long while and many difficult episodes, pitched emotional battles, and hours of reflection to arrive at an equilibrium that satisfied the various demands on my ability to be a caregiver.

Over the years of being a stepmom, I was faced with some particularly difficult challenges for which I was not remotely prepared. The boys' biological mother had left them when they were very young. The price they paid for this abandonment and the uncertainty it caused included loss of self-esteem and constant battles with many demons. In the early years, though, after a period of initial readjustment, family life with my three stepsons was pretty normal. They went to good schools, we went on vacations at the lake where I had gone with Marcia, and we spent holidays together. In every way, we were a family.

It was only when the boys became teenagers that the latent problems began to surface, especially when one day, fifteen years after leaving them, their biological mother reappeared out of the blue. I can only guess at her motives, but suffice it to say her reemergence into our lives had the same impact as a hurricane hitting town, because the boys—and our family—were suddenly emotionally shorn in two. With their birth mother's reentry into their lives, the boys at first thought they had found nirvana. Moreover, their mother soon convinced them that I was an obstacle to their reunion as a family.

I was, of course, stunned, shocked, hurt, angry, upset, and confused. How, after having devoted fifteen years of my life to doing the best I could, how *could* this have come to pass? After all, nothing had changed about *my* feelings toward my sons. To me, they were my children. I loved them, and my love for them never wavered, no matter what they said or did. I would have done *anything* to keep them safe because, to me, they were *my* boys. In my weakest moments, when self-pity raised its sullen head, I would feel persecuted and angry that my love and caregiving had been disregarded or, worse, betrayed. But those moments would pass quickly when my instinct to love and care for my boys and others would reassert its rightful place in my heart and mind. Still, I didn't remotely understand the dynamics that were ruining our family, because when you are in the middle of something that threatens your survival, as we were, it is always hard to see beyond the immediate need to survive.

This, again, is one of the paramount dangers that all caregivers face: when you identify too closely with your subject, you cannot be objective about him or her—or about yourself. The dilemma, of course, is to find that equilibrium in the relationship that lets you give care without letting that caregiving overwhelm you. If you are unsuccessful in this search to find a balance, however, the result can be, and usually *is*, corrosive. A vicious circle is established in which boundaries are routinely bent or broken until a crisis of some sort facilitates a resolution.

Casting about for answers, I turned to what I had learned in the past and to the lessons I had gotten from Marcia—in particular, to the lesson that I had to *acknowledge and learn from adversity.* I will admit, however, that this was not as easy as it sounds. I was emotionally shattered and needed to unwrap this gift again and again in order to focus all my strength to get through this gut-wrenching period when my boys were totally rejecting me. But with the experience of getting on my hands and knees after school and helping Marcia learn to crawl foremost in my mind, I was determined that I was going to transform this tragedy into new strengths, just as Marcia had learned to walk with our help. With help from my friends, especially some female ones (whom I call my "goal friends"), I learned to look, with open eyes, at the past fifteen years of my life and to see where I had lost sight of myself, how I had ignored things that were in front of me, and how I had gotten lost.

In this process of rediscovery, I went back, in order to help find my core-self, to all the other gifts Marcia had given me. There were many questions I asked myself: Did I, for instance, allow each boy to be unique as he grew up? Did I try to help each one identify his *own unique ability*, whether it was a creative one, an athletic one, or an intellectual one? Did I teach them it was okay to be different? Did I try to teach them to *discover their own purpose in life*? Did I support each one of them? Was I honest? Did I *treasure the truth* about them? Did I teach them how to *acknowledge and learn from the adversity* they had faced in their young lives already? Did I now *value the importance of independence* to them? Was I able to let them know that I *cherished and loved them*? Had I given the boys a nourishing childhood over those fifteen years? Would they, over time, understand and believe in my love for them?

But just as I was beginning to answer some of these questions and was coming to terms with the boys' needs to go their own ways, at least for a time, my life was turned upside down once again. One day, while in a business meeting, I was interrupted with an emergency phone call. The message was that my middle stepson had shot himself, was in the hospital, and was not expected to live.

I put my faith in what I had learned from Marcia, to let people (including myself) do what they can according to their strengths and accept their contributions as being indicative of the best they have to offer. Being a caregiver in the situation I was in, I could only do as much as I was allowed to do. I could only tell my son I loved him and show as best I could that I cared about him, knowing that the impact of my care would be felt by him eventually. I prayed, having to rely upon the medical professionals to heal my son. The amazing result was that he recovered and eventually walked out of the hospital.

As time went by, I continued to maintain contact with all three of my sons, no matter what form that contact took. Sometimes, I called my sons and would get no response for a month or more. But when I did get a call back, I treasured the moment, knowing that it could be some time before I would hear from them again. Every time we would speak, I would tell them how much I loved them, as Marcia had done with us throughout her life. I had faith that if I applied this lesson I learned from Marcia, with patience, in the end, things *would* work out the way they should. Through all of this I have learned, with Marcia's help, that love, appreciation, patience, and faith are the four prime ingredients of hope. I continue to appreciate every day for the singular moment in time that it is, love those people in my life whom I treasure, have faith that the promise of the future is being sown every day, and have patience that if I tend to my life with care, all things will come to pass.

As evidence of my faith that the seeds of hope are being planted and reaching fruition every day, life has taken a positive turn, as I once again have a positive familial and loving relationship with all three of my boys. And it is encouraging to see that the stepson who was injured, though now blinded for life, is at last on a path of redemption. That is, he is learning Braille and other living skills tailored for the blind. Most importantly, he has acquired a fresh, and far healthier, outlook on living. Yes, it took a terrible toll on him, but the crisis in his life has also given him a lucidity that has helped him free himself of the issues that kept him bound to the past. The road ahead for him may prove to be a difficult one, but the course he is undertaking is finally pointing in a direction that will, I hope, lead him to happiness and love. As he said to me recently, "Mom, before, I could not really see. But now that I am blind, I can see clearer." So, in my mind, I feel that the roads my sons and I have traveled have been in some ways parallel, and also that they have been made a little easier because of the lessons Marcia taught me.

***

Caregiving as a Daughter
The Oldest Daughter's Duty

In answer to the question I posed earlier—about whether we can truly learn from others the anguish they feel without experiencing it ourselves—I said that the most difficult lessons cannot be shared, only experienced. I would like to share with you, as best I can, my experience—and my anguish—in having to make the same decisions about my parents' care that they had to make about Marcia's. As in my role as stepmother, the role of being a caregiver to aging parents tested the same limits of my caregiving abilities and highlighted the difficulty of putting the lessons I had learned from them and Marcia into practice.

First of all, let me say that my parents were phenomenal people. They were not wealthy, but my mother and father never let their children know they struggled financially. Scrambled eggs, pancakes, and fish sticks were acceptable dinners. Doing our share of the household chores was part of life. Getting a babysitting job if I really wanted that new coat was the status quo. The expectation to always get great grades in school was the norm. Sunday night was popcorn night for all. Vacation was a day at the beach on a summer's Sunday, if we could afford it.

Those beach trips really were a treat. Mom would make her "special" fried chicken, potato salad, and lemonade, and then all eight of us would pile into the old Kaiser, and off we would go to Cedar Lake. Of course, Dad would *always* get lost and would never think of asking for directions. The roof liner of the car would capture air inside it if he drove too fast, and the cloth ceiling material would billow out like a sail and press down on our heads as he drove. We also *always* seemed to get stuck in the mud every time we exited the parking lot of the beach. But this was our vacation, and we treasured it. Babysitting our siblings was also the norm, and if one sister just happened to need some extra medications or help, that was just the way of our lives. We all learned a sense of responsibility from day one. We all grew up feeling that increased responsibility itself was the reward.

When our mother started forgetting things little by little, we were too busy with our own lives to notice. She was busy, after all, and we just assumed our lives would go on normally as they always had. When Marcia died, our mother, unknown to us, lost not only her daughter, but she also began losing her memories—of Marcia, of us, of her life— to the silent, cruel, unseen, and inexorable workings of dementia. We will never know, but perhaps the responsibility of caring for Marcia had forestalled its onset until after her death. In any case, after Marcia was gone, it grew apparent to us that Mom was having trouble holding onto thoughts and was forgetting things.

Making dinner one Sunday, for instance, she couldn't find the ham she had bought, which she swore she had put in the freezer, so she just prepared something else. When we found the ham several months later in the storage bin in the basement—with the cleaning supplies—we started to wonder what was going on. (Yes, we found the ham with our noses!) As Mom forgot more and more, she would become upset with her inability to recall things she wanted to tell us or things she had forgotten to do. She had less patience with my father and sometimes threatened him with eviction to the garage for slight offenses. We thought she was teasing, but as I look back, I realize she might have meant it. She must have been sensing that she needed to assert herself in any way possible in order to stem the insidious loss of control she was experiencing. I can only imagine the degree of terror she must also have been enduring at her inability to remember things she had long taken for granted. At the time, our denial and her stoicism led us to ignore the fact that any of this was occurring.

One day, I asked her about the time she met my father. My mother had gone to a picnic with "Frank," but at the picnic, she met my father, left Frank, and went home with my father. It was an endearing story, and I had always loved hearing her relate it to me. But this particular day, she couldn't recall the story. I thought she was kidding me, in the way she sometimes did, making fun of the fact that she had actually "dumped" Frank for my dad. Only days later did I come to the realization that she had *not* been teasing me. She actually had *not been able to remember* this story, which was one of the cornerstones of her life. To forget something so central to her past was inconceivable to me, and it caused me to acknowledge the problem for the first time. Initially, I kept my concerns to myself. The potential enormity of mom's condition frightened me. With this acknowledgement of my mother's deterioration came the inescapable knowledge and the expectation that the worst was yet to come.

Indeed, my own worst fears were realized soon enough. Mom, I discovered, could no longer remember how to do basic chores, like laundry. What came first when loading the washing machine: the soap, the water, or the clothes? Her ability to cook dinner also dissolved. Unable to cope with the issue directly, and unwilling to admit what we all knew separately, we were afraid to share with each other. We kept trying to make excuses for Mom. She had cooked for years and years, which was long enough. She was just sending us a message that she had

had enough of housecleaning. She was tired. It was our turn to do the housecleaning, cooking, and laundry.

A point of no return that we all recognized came one Thanksgiving, when brave faces and excuses could no longer give lie to our private secret or to our rationalization that she was merely fatigued.

Thanksgiving was always my mother's holiday. She loved all the preparations. As she got older, she would make the side dishes, and I would bring the turkey and prepare it for her. A tradition developed. On the evening before Thanksgiving this one year, my stepson Timothy and I went to "Grandma's" to prepare dinner for the next day with her. However, when we arrived, my father let me know that my mother had already been cooking—*for months*!

He was right. The refrigerator was full of side dishes, which had been prepared months in advance. I was dumbfounded. Dad had to have known what Mom had been up to. What had he thought? Why hadn't he said anything to her? Why hadn't he mentioned this earlier to us? Although the word "dementia" was never spoken that day, even my father could not hide the truth from himself any longer. His wife, our mother, was losing her memory and losing control of her ability to take care of herself, let alone take care of the rest of us.

Not wanting to confront my mother with what we knew, in part because we didn't actually know *what* to do with our knowledge, Tim and I talked Dad into taking Mom out for a few hours. Tim and I cleaned out the months-old food and re-prepared the side dishes in the *exact-same bowls* so Mom wouldn't know, and we had a wonderful dinner the next day. In doing this we avoided a crisis, but we knew we had come to a fork in the road, and the destination of that road for my mother was too painful for us to deal with directly on Thanksgiving. So, when it came time to say grace before dinner, Tim, his eyes moist and his voice quivering, said nothing about the score of side dishes thawing in the trash cans outside. Instead, he gave thanks to Grandma for cooking such a wonderful dinner. I could have wept. My heart (and Tim's and Dad's, too, I suspect) was breaking with each word, with each bite of the holiday feast, because we suspected this would be Grandma's last remembered Thanksgiving dinner.

My mother's condition had been given a name, finally. It progressed inexorably, but even though it was obvious to everyone now that Mom had vascular dementia, my father was still not prepared to accept it. He was sure there was some type of medicine to make her better. There must be help for his mate. One day, when my mother could not get out of the bathtub alone, my father had to call the fire department for help. Still, he did not accept that she needed outside assistance. He would accept only that perhaps she "might need some more medicine." But even in this, he was slow to act and would not let us take her to see a new doctor, because he didn't want to hurt their doctor's feelings. So, in fact, we did not make that change until the old doctor retired.

Dad did not cook, so we tried to have Meals On Wheels help. But he didn't like their food, so we tried other home-delivery services. But he tired quickly of that food, too. He did, however, like the food that his daughters brought him. *Of course*! All of us encouraged him to have a caregiver come in to help him cook, but that, too, was resisted. He finally did agree to let a caregiver come in for a few hours a day, but since the person didn't do things *his* way, that just frustrated my father even more.

Daily I would stop at my parents' home and check on them. I would find my mother wet, sometimes dirty, hungry, and frustrated. That was on a *good* day. She still knew enough to know that something was wrong, but she could no longer find the words to describe what it was. Despite the deterioration of Mom's care, Dad still refused a caregiver. "Why do you think I had so many daughters?" was his semi-combative response to my prodding. So, we kept trying to make it work.

Then Dad started to lose capacity himself. He had emphysema and macular degeneration. He needed to have oxygen more and more often, and his vision was failing. He still insisted that he could drive, even though he had to take his oxygen tank with him, and he insisted that he could take care of my mother. My father was a stubborn man. He was also a proud man.

From Marcia, I had already learned how important independence is to all of us, so I tried to honor my father's wishes. Then, we tried a different tack: we encouraged him to hire a caregiver "for Mom." Only after my mother could no longer get out of bed by herself and could no longer swallow solid food did my father finally relent and start to acknowledge that he needed help—but only "for Mom," not for himself.

With his permission, we interviewed caregivers and were ready to hire one. As we sat one Sunday afternoon, talking about the caregiver who had been selected, my father suddenly grew very angry at us, his grown children. "You've no right to take my right to live on my own away from me! I can do this alone! I don't need any help!" he stormed. When he calmed down a while later, after we had called the caregiver and apologized to her that we wouldn't need her services after all, he admitted, "I'm just not ready yet."

But whether he was ready or not, the need increased. Mom could no longer dress herself. She could not feed herself. Nor could she bathe herself. Finally acknowledging the inevitable, Dad gave in. He agreed to hire a caregiver to help Mom. *But not one for him!*

The caregiver prepared Mom's meals, bathed her and dressed her, and if there *just happened* to be some food left over that Dad could eat, well, that was great. Our parents' care needs were at last being met. It was a tremendous relief for us. We managed to get along in this manner for quite some time, as things settled into predictable routines. Eventually, Dad's condition got worse, too. He could no longer take care of the house, himself, or my mother—yet he still refused care for himself from anyone except his children.

I hired an elder-care consultant to come in and review the house situation. She recommended I get a hospital bed for Dad to help him sleep comfortably. I shared her recommendation with my father, and he initially agreed. However, as he thought about it for a day or two, he became agitated. The evening before the bed was to arrive, he told me he didn't want it. He said that if the bed came into his house, he would just sleep in the basement. (Of course, he had forgotten that he could no longer make it down to the basement without significant help.) "I'm not an invalid, after all," he hollered at me. Being my father's daughter and frustrated to tears, I yelled back at him, "You don't love Mom! Because if you did, you would do things for her that would keep her safe!"

I left in tears, swearing to myself that I was done with caregiving. I got on the phone and called my brother Ron in Peoria, saying I couldn't do it another day.

But I did go back. The next day.

My father and I never talked about the hospital bed again, and it was taken away. That day, though, I relearned the lesson I had learned from Marcia but had forgotten: acknowledge and learn from adversity. That is, if I was going to help my father, I needed to respect his wishes, make him comfortable in whatever way he would allow me, and accept it. I could not put my values on him nor expect him to change at the age of ninety-one.

My father finally succumbed to his illness, but not before leaving his legacy. Those last days of his were ones I will never forget. The experience of, and around, my father's death had a profound impact on me and, because it tested every fiber of my being, it is one that I can never leave behind.

It was Saturday, December 14th, the day of my company's holiday party. I was having all of my employees and their spouses to my home for dinner. We had planned a wonderful event. The house and yard were decorated to the nines. The tree was gorgeous; its base was knee-deep in gift packages for the boys. That morning, my brother called. He said he did not think Dad would make it through the day. Moreover, he confided that Dad didn't want me to know how bad the situation was because he knew it was the day of my party, and he didn't want to spoil it. My brother made me promise not to tell Dad that he had called me. (As if Dad wouldn't know, since he had his full mental capacities right to the very end.)

Well, let me say that there was *nothing* on earth that could have kept me from seeing my father on what I thought was going to the last day of his life—not even if I went against his wish that I go to my party! I called my husband to let him know I would not be at the party and asked if he could be the host that evening. There was no question in my mind that I had to be with my dad, and I knew my employees would understand.

As it happened, my father passed away peacefully three days later, with me at his side moments before his actual passing. Before he slipped away, though, we talked. We talked about his life. We talked about his regrets. We talked about his wishes for his family. We talked about how happy he had been with my mother. We talked about how proud he was of us children. He wrapped up this conversation—the final one of his life—with a few last-minute instructions, as he always did:

"Keep your mother safe, don't pay the guy who cuts the grass more than twenty-five dollars, and don't pay the guy who shovels the snow more than twenty."

Once a dad, always a dad.

His next-to-last words to me were that he would find Marcia after he died and would say hi to her for me. "You'll know whenever I'm with her," he whispered, "because your hair will stand straight up on end on the top of your head." And he smiled at me that smile he had, through the gasps for air, as he tried to stay with us.

Even though I didn't want to lose my father and still felt I needed him, I chuckled as he spoke these words, for I thought that he was teasing me as usual (although I'm sure now that he was trying only to comfort me and ease my sadness, since I had wept all through that day). He then surprised me. "I wish for you," he murmured, emphasizing the last word, "that you will find someone who will take care of *you*."

I said a final goodbye to my father, and then his new journey began peacefully. He died shortly after that final goodbye. I thank God for having granted me the opportunity to spend these precious last moments with Dad. I count myself blessed to have had the privilege of seeing him off on his voyage to go stand before his God.

One of the things, apart from my work, that helped most in the grieving for my dad was the caregiving I provided for my mother. Somehow, knowing I was making sure my mother was safe made *me* feel safe, too. However, as caregiving for parents can go, not everything goes as planned. One setback, for instance, came when a hired caregiver had left Mom home alone, locked in the house while she went to dinner with her husband. This potentially fatal lapse in her judgment infuriated me beyond imagining. This indignation was, in turn, channeled positively into resolve, on my part, to find another caregiver, one with firmer ethical standards. Blessedly, the next caregiver I hired was extraordinary.

Once this particular setback was overcome and my mother was safe again, I continued working on "finding myself". It took some serious inner revelations to understand what my dad had been trying to tell me on the last day of his life: *that I needed to find someone to take care of me.*

I have since learned that what Dad meant was that, at the end of the day, the only one who can take care of me is *me*. In other words, The adage "Heal thyself, physician" applies. To repeat myself, the first truth of any caregiver, whether it's a triage nurse or an airline flight attendant, is to take care of him- or herself so that he or she may care for others. Taking this to heart, I now work at making sure that I do what I need to do to stay healthy, both physically and mentally, for I am truly no good to anyone who might need me if I myself am not okay.

Throughout this entire experience, the gifts Marcia had left allowed me to remain intact physically, mentally, and emotionally. I focused on cherishing every day. Most importantly, I continued to believe my purpose was to be a caregiver and that my duty was to learn from this entire life experience and to try to teach others the lessons I was learning.

My mother continued to lose mental and physical capacity and required nursing-home care. The decision to place my mother in a nursing home was one of the most difficult decisions I have ever faced, and I have some sense now about how my parents must have felt when Marcia went to Clearbrook. Not surprisingly, the process of looking for a nursing facility and selling the family home, handling the details, cleaning the house, taking care of Mom whenever the caregiver needed a day off, and taking care of the bills and documentation came back to the same siblings who were there for Marcia's support. That is, having learned from that earlier experience, I was not at all surprised about who was willing and able to do what. Although there were times when, I will admit, it was difficult, once again, thanks to Marcia, I recognize we are all different beings and, as we did with Marcia, we used our varying talents in divergent ways to show our love and concern for our mother. So often I hear from clients how one or two siblings might resent having to be the ones with the "responsibility," and I try to explain that someday, they *will* look back and be thankful for this opportunity to be the caregiver. It is just hard to imagine when one is in the thick of things.

I visited Mom at least every few days. Although she no longer knew me as her daughter, I still knew her as my mother. The lesson of cherishing every day came to mind whenever I saw her. My mother no longer conversed with me, but once in a long while she would say one sentence, or one *word*, out of the blue. Every time I told her I loved her, she said it back to me with her eyes. Even though my mother didn't recognize me, I do believe she felt my love and returned it tenfold. Perhaps, somewhere in her brain and in her heart, she knew she was making me happy by allowing me to continue on as a caregiver. This is all that a caregiver can hope for, that his or her work is making an impact, even though it may not be immediately apparent or acknowledged. My mother passed away on Easter Sunday, just a few months ago, and my siblings and I all had the knowledge that we cared for her to the best of our abilities throughout her dementia, and that gave us the peace we needed.

My mother's passing was the end of one of the segments of my journey. It was not a direct route, but it, too, resulted in a destination that will change my life once again. Now, many mornings when I wake up, I feel refreshed in my new life. Quite frequently, when I wake up after a night's sleep, I notice the hair on my head is standing straight up! It is at those times when I can hear most clearly my father's voice in my heart saying hi to Marcia—and to me. And I feel Marcia's arms wrap around me and her laughter spread through my heart.

The Gifts Revisited

"Marcia gave each of us so much love.
Oh, to only have her with me one more day!"

~ Helen Wallace

The gift that Marcia gave to me is priceless. This gift was in one big box, wrapped in a beautiful bow. As I opened it, it held many smaller boxes. You see, Marcia loved to unwrap gifts! It is impossible to list these gifts in order of importance, since one lesson often depends upon another. Be that as it may, here is my list of six gifts I have received from Marcia, which I have tried to apply to my life and to my work:

1. **Embrace Diversity**: Everyone has a unique ability; everyone has at least one disability. The important thing in life is to focus on the gift of one's unique ability. When I am totally frustrated that someone isn't doing his or her share or doing things the way I think they should be done, I have to *get over it*. We are all different.

2. **Discover Your Purpose**: We all have a purpose. We just need to search for it, recognize it, and embrace it. Our purpose may vary at times, but we do know when we are doing what we were made to be doing.

3. **Treasure the Truth**: Honesty is a value that cannot be replaced with any other value. It is something that all other facts are based on; it has its own reward. At times, it would be easier to not be honest with myself, because the hardest person to be honest with is me, but I find this is key to my feeling safe. Much to the chagrin of my friends, I will say how I feel and hope they understand. Marcia just doesn't let me do otherwise.

4. **Acknowledge and Learn from Adversity**: When I thought I could not go on, I learned to transform tragedies in my life to lessons and strengths. There were days when I wanted to give up, but I have learned that if I want to make it through the tough times, I must make time and find a place for self-reflection. Each time adversity seemed to come into my life, I came out on the other side of it as a stronger, more enlightened person.

5. **Value the Importance of Independence**: No matter how much help we might need, we grow and learn through achieving independence. Understanding when to ask for help and when to stand on one's own is a fine balance and a worthy achievement in and of itself. Self-esteem achieved through independence is priceless.

6. **Cherish Each and Every Day**: Appreciate every day. There is an endless supply of things in life that we can fret over, but they are not all that important in the big picture. This

isn't to say I don't fret. Everyone who knows me will say otherwise. But I work hard at staying in the present so that I can appreciate where I am, who I am with, and why I am there at the moment. My view on life has been forever changed by Marcia. Life is short. Stay in the present.

Each one of these topics could fill a book. My hope is that people who take the time to read this book will look within their own experiences for similar lessons they might have learned. Marcia inspired me to discover what I do best. She taught me that life is a journey, and if I embrace the entire journey, there will be an "Ah Ha!" at the end.

I hope that the following chapters provide a road map for other caregivers, no matter what type of caregiver you may be. Caregiving transcends generations. Many of us find ourselves caring for children while also caring for our parents. This dynamic will only increase over time. As more and more baby boomers take on the responsibility of caring for their parents, their children, and maybe even a sibling, the step by step approach that follows becomes critical to our own peace of mind. I wish you a safe journey over the many roads you will travel and hope that you too will find the "Ah Ha" in your caregiving role. As this book helps you on your journey, you have Marcia to thank.

The Eight Steps to
Protected Tomorrows

The process of learning from Marcia—from the day she was born to beyond her death—and the process of providing the care for my parents and stepchildren has brought me untold rewards that I can never fully repay. As a start, I have committed myself to helping families with individuals with disabilities as well as caring for the elderly. Over the years, this has taken form in the services provided by my planning company. By trial and error, through countless hours of work spanning over almost twenty years, we have accomplished much that I am proud of. We have also learned many things about providing advocacy services for persons needing care.

Given our experience, we have been able to refine some of the wisdom and experience that we have accrued into a process called the Process for Protected Tomorrows. The diagram at the end of this section illustrates the basic steps by which we can execute any plan. To get started on planning, you might take the following steps. Each step comes with a separate worksheet you can utilize to guide you along the process. You can also find updated printable copies of each worksheet on our website, www.protectedtomorrows.com, along with resources to make your caregiving role a little easier. Each step defined in this book will direct you to the proper online page to find the worksheets you need. Make sure you select the proper worksheet, depending upon if you are the caregiver for a person with a disability or for a parent or other senior.

Don't become overwhelmed. Take one step at a time. Ask for help along the way. We are here to help guide you as you take each road on the journey. If you reach a fork in the road, you feel alone, and don't know which way to turn, contact us. We are here for you. Let's get started with **Step One: Take a Candid Look™**. You start this very step by asking yourself questions. Try to step back and make an honest appraisal of your loved one's future needs. Families have hectic lives. Those families who have an individual needing care have demands placed on them that are typically beyond the norm. Beyond looking for the best schools, care facilities and homes, jobs, and overall support for their families, families with special needs have to be constant advocates. But the first step is to be honest. Very, very honest.

Consider the following questions:

✓ What are the limitations of the person with the disability?
✓ What are the unique abilities of the person with the disability?
✓ Have you even yet *admitted* that the person may have some limitations?
✓ What are your dreams for this family member?

✓ What are the dangers he or she will face in the years to come?

✓ What opportunities do you think this family member might have?

✓ Do you think often enough about the abilities, rather than the disabilities, so that you can truly help the person focus on his or her strengths?

✓ How do you set aside the time to fit this into your already-overwhelming life?

✓ What about *you*? Are you taking care of *you*?

All of these questions must first be answered candidly if you want to make progress in your planning for today and the future.

Start this step by completing the Step 1 Worksheet, called Take a Candid Look. A worksheet appears on the next page.

Special Book Offer: Obtain the most current version of this worksheet online at www.protectedtomorrows.com/bookoffer.

PROTECTED TOMORROWS®   Take a Candid Look™ - *All*

1

Person Requiring Care: _____   Date: _____

Caregiver(s): _____

This may be the first time you address head on the dreams, goals, and fears you have for your loved one. However, it is worth taking some time to think through it. This is the first step in starting to recognize the steps you must take to achieve peace of mind. Make an honest appraisal of all future care needs in light of the entire family's make up and financial situation.

What stage of your caregiving journey are you on?

What Now?   (I don't even know where to start?)

Why Me?   (I've started, but I feel so alone and confused!)

Ah Ha!   (I think I know what I'm doing, but need more help.)

Describe your Current Situation

What can your loved one do for him/herself? What are their limitations? What facts do you have now? Who is helping you? Be truly honest as to what is facing you today.

Concerns & Fears

What keeps you up at night about providing the proper care for your loved one? What dangers is your loved one facing? Can you keep them safe and happy?

Dreams & Goals

What would be the best thing that could happen if you could do the best caregiving job possible? Describe your vision for how you would like to see things in a year from today.

Step Two: Create the Future Map™. Identify the vision you have for the person's life, including opportunities and obstacles. Create a plan to protect your entire extended family's future. You must identify the different stages of life and, within each stage, express what you see as the residential, educational, recreational, and employment options. Each of these areas presents both opportunities and challenges for all of us, but you need to create a plan that not only addresses these areas in the different stages of life, but one that is also dynamic. Remember, none of us can foretell the future, so expect your Future Map to be a flexible document. Make sure you select the proper worksheet depending upon who you are caring for (person with a disability or parent or senior).

   ✓ Identify the different stages that you want to design.
   ✓ For each of these stages, develop a scenario of how you think life will look for your family member. Define this in as much detail as you now have, as this will be the base upon which you build in the future.
   ✓ For each of the scenarios, identify what you don't know, so that you can begin researching opportunities with very specific goal dates as to when you will look for this information.
   ✓ Don't become overwhelmed. The first time you attempt this, stay at a high level. As you continue to build upon each scenario, it will become clearer.

Start this step by completing the correct Step 2 Worksheet, called Create the Future Map. Worksheets appear on the next two pages.

Special Book Offer: Obtain the most current version of these worksheets online at www.protectedtomorrows.com/bookoffer.

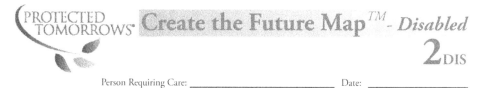

PROTECTED TOMORROWS® **Create the Future Map**^{TM} - *Disabled*

2DIS

Person Requiring Care: _____ Date: _____

Caregiver(s): _____

Identify all life needs including quality of life supports, medical needs, residential settings, educational supports, wellness programs, and recreational activities, based upon the individual's ability to support him or herself in these activities. The family/caregivers develop a vision of what they see for the individual in the different stages of his/her life. Then you can quantify the cash flow required to support these living needs, as well as the amount of income and corresponding assets that are necessary.

# of years in each stage					
Annual Income	School Years	High School	Transition	Adulthood	Life Without You
* Work					
* Social Security/ Other Gov't Programs					
* Family					
* Other					
TOTAL					
Annual Expenses	School Years	High School	Transition	Adulthood	Life Without You
* Living					
* Medical					
* Recreation					
* Education					
* Work					
* Taxes					
TOTAL					
Net Need (Income – Expenses)					
Need X Number of Years in Stage					

Create the Future Map™ - *Senior*

2_{SR}

Person Requiring Care: _____ Date: _____

Caregiver(s): _____

The family/caregivers develop a vision of what they see for the individual in the different stages of his/her life. Identify all life needs including quality of life supports, medical needs, residential settings, wellness programs, and recreational activities, based upon the individual's ability to support him or herself in these activities. Then you can quantify the cash flow required to support these living needs, as well as the amount of income and corresponding assets that are necessary.

# of years in each stage					
Annual Income	School Years	High School	Transition	Adulthood	Life Without You
* Work					
* Social Security/ Other Gov't Programs					
* Pension					
* Family					
* Other					
TOTAL					
Annual Expenses	School Years	High School	Transition	Adulthood	Life Without You
* Living					
* Medical					
* Recreation					
* Education					
* Work					
* Taxes					
TOTAL					
Net Need (Income – Expenses)					
Need X Number of Years in Stage					

Step Three: Filter the Legal Options™. Many families want to delay this portion of their planning. Thinking about death is not pleasant. In a family with special needs, we truly want to put off thinking about this. The thought of not being around forever to keep someone safe is so overwhelming, it is just easier to delay this step. The legal process can be confusing. Even hearing the word "trust" can be a little scary for some. But this process does not need to be daunting. Let's start with just a few definitions:

Third Party Discretionary Supplemental Needs Trust: If a family wishes to provide for a family member with a disability through an inheritance, there is a way to leave assets in a trust that will not disqualify the person with the disability from receiving certain government benefits. A special needs trust can hold cash, personal property, real property, or can be the beneficiary of life insurance proceeds. Simply stated, other people's money or property that they choose to contribute or leave to someone with disabilities can be set aside safely to provide for the supplemental care for the future of person with the disability.

First Party Discretionary Supplemental Care Trust or Payback Trust: If a person under the age of 65 has assets that disqualifies him/her from receiving government benefits a Payback Trust can be created that can hold cash, personal property or real property that is owned by the person with disabilities. This can only be set up by parents, grandparents, legal guardians or the court. This trust also has very specific rules that must be followed, and it differs from the Third Party trust in that it must have a payback provision, so that the state is paid back for medical expenses paid, at the death of the beneficiary.

For each of these legal documents as well as other planning such as wills and guardianship, some decisions need to be made. If you can take things one step at a time, you will give yourself time to think about the decisions you need to make without putting the legalese into the picture. Consider the following:

<u>Who are the "Money People</u>™"? Who will help the individual with special needs pay bills, manage money, and help with other business and bureaucratic responsibilities? Who would you trust to do this? If you can't think of anyone, take a few minutes to jot down everyone you know who is good with money. Circle the top three names that you think might help. Put them in order now from one to three.

Who are the "Future Care People™"? Who besides you will be there for your family member with special needs? Who inquires about their safety and best interests? Who would you trust to stay with your family member if you had an emergency? This is usually the toughest part of this step. You are identifying someone to whom you are giving *your* job. It could be a lifetime job for him or her. Because this step is so difficult, most caregivers procrastinate and just don't face it. Again, take out a piece of paper, write down all of those persons you know who are caring. Now, which of those persons care about your child? Circle the top three names. Now put them in order from one to three.

How do you find the right attorney to help you? What resources are available that can direct you? Using the wrong attorney can be devastating to your estate plan, and it will waste your precious time. If you can't find an attorney who does special needs work in your area, check out our website at www.protectedtomorrows.com for some assistance.

Are you planning for your parents? Ask yourself if they still have competence to make their own decisions. If not, special planning must take place for you to assist them.

None of these are easy decisions, but they are important ones that must be made—and they must be made *now*. Waiting will not make them any easier, and it puts your family member at risk if something happens to you.

Start this step by completing the proper Step 3 Worksheet, called Filter the Legal Option. Worksheets appear on the next two pages.

Special Book Offer: Obtain the most current version of these worksheets online at www.protectedtomorrows.com/bookoffer.

Filter the Legal Options™ - *Disabled*

3DIS

Person Requiring Care: _____ Date: _____

Caregiver(s): _____

Legal considerations are an important part of the process. Certain legal documents are critical and can assist in speeding up or slowing down care for your loved one. There are many components to planning, which may include wills, powers of attorney, Living Trusts and perhaps a Special Needs Trust. Guardianship/Conservatorship might also need to be considered. Finding legal counsel who understands the specifics of drafting these types of documents is important. Before seeing an attorney, gather any existing documents, have a concise listing of assets and liabilities, and think through the many decisions that will need to be made. This step will help make the time with the attorney most efficient.

What estate planning documents do you as the parents/caregivers currently have?

Wills   Power of Attorney for Health Care
Living Trusts   Power of Attorney for Property
Special Needs Trust   Other

Do you understand the usage of a Special Needs Trust?

Yes, I totally understand it.
Yes, but would like to know more.
No, I need to learn.
(To learn more, go to *www.protectedtomorrows.com/bookoffer*)

The trustee I have selected for the Special Needs Trust (or will select) are:

First Choice:

Second Choice:

Third Choice:

Are you the guardian for your family member with a disability?

Yes, and I understand what my job entails.
Yes, but I'm not sure what I am to be doing.
I am not sure.
No. Do I need to be?
(To learn more, go to *www.protectedtomorrows.com/bookoffer*)

The future guardians I have selected (or will select) are:

First Choice:

Second Choice:

Third Choice:

Have you prepared the future guardians with the information they need to know?
(See *www.protectedtomorrows.com/bookoffer*)

Filter the Legal Options™ - Senior

3_{SR}

Person Need Care: _____ Date: _____

Caregiver(s): _____

Legal considerations are an important part of the process. Certain legal documents are critical and can assist in speeding up or slowing down care for your loved one. There are many components to planning, which may include wills, powers of attorney, Living Trusts and perhaps a Special Needs Trust. Guardianship/Conservatorship might also need to be considered. Finding legal counsel who understands the specifics of drafting these types of documents is important. Before seeing an attorney, gather any existing documents, have a concise listing of assets and liabilities, and think through the many decisions that will need to be made. This step will help make the time with the attorney most efficient.

What estate planning documents does the person needing care have?

Wills
Living Trusts
Special Needs Trust

Power of Attorney for Health Care
Power of Attorney for Property
Other

Are you the agent on the powers of attorney and/or successor trustee?

Yes.
No. (If No, does the person have current capacity to sign new powers?)
        Yes   No

Do you have a current list of all assets and liabilities for the individual?

Yes.
No. I'm working on it.

Are there other family members/friends who are helping you provide the care?

Yes. If Yes, List Names:
No.

Where is the individual currently living?

At Home
With Me
Independent Living

Assisted Living
Nursing Home

Find an Advocate and an Attorney

Go to *www.protectedtomorrows.com/bookoffer*
Look up a Protected Tomorrows Advocate and an Estate Planning Attorney
in your area, who can help you with the next steps.

Step Four: Capture Potential Benefits™. Identify sources of income and assets available that will provide care for your loved one. This may include social services, community assistance and government programs that will enhance and support the future care plan, including special doctors, schools, recreational programs, and even research protocols. If something were to happen to you, how much do you really need to leave for a family member with special needs? If it is his or her own money, is it enough? Is it positioned properly? If you are planning to be around for a very long time, how do you make sure you can provide your family member with a decent quality of life, even if you cannot afford to subsidize him or her? Are there steps you should be taking now to ensure you are not undoing benefits that might be available? Are you aware of the rules? Do you know how to access resources that will keep you abreast of changes to the rules? You need to become an advocate for your family member, make sure you know the rules, or hire someone to help you. Don't take it for granted that your family member will receive assistance. Be careful not to make a mistake out of ignorance. Yes, ignorance is bliss, but bliss is not a luxury you can afford. Get some help if this step is overwhelming.

Government benefits eligibility is key to financial security, as well as important to meeting healthcare, residential, vocational and recreational needs. The government defines a disability in a number of ways, depending on what programs a client needs. According to the U.S. Department of Labor's Office of Disability Employment Policy, disability is a person who has a physical or mental impairment that substantially limits one or more major life activities. For Social Security disability benefits, individuals must have a severe disability (or combination of disabilities) that has lasted, or is expected to last, at least 12 months; and to obtain state vocational rehabilitation services, a person must have a physical or mental impairment that constitutes or results in a "substantial impediment" to employment for the applicant. Furthermore, the individual must be deemed disabled under Social Security to get Medicare/Medicaid health insurance services.

Here are more detailed explanations for the government benefits one might be eligible for.

Supplemental Security Income (SSI): A Federal income supplement program funded by general tax revenues (*not* Social

Security taxes). Its purpose is to help the aged, blind and disabled who have little or no income. It currently provides a maximum amount per month to be used for basic needs such as food, clothing and shelter. This amount typically increases annually. It is generally for people who have little or no work history.

Social Security Disability Insurance (SSDI): A federal cash benefit that may be available if a person is disabled. It pays benefits to the individual and certain members of the individual's family if they are "insured," meaning they worked long enough and paid Social Security taxes.

Medicare: A federal health insurance program for people 65 years of age or older, certain younger people with disabilities, and people with End-Stage Renal Disease (permanent kidney failure with dialysis or a transplant). Medicare does not cover everything, and it does not pay the total cost for most services or supplies that are covered.

Medicaid: A program that provides medical assistance for certain individuals and families with low incomes and resources. Medicaid eligibility is limited to individuals who fall into specific categories. Although the Federal government establishes general guidelines, the Medicaid program requirements are actually established by each state. In addition to paying for some medical services and prescriptions, Medicaid may also pay for residential facilities, workshops, job coaches and other very important programs.

It's important to evaluate your family member's entire life picture and take a few more things into consideration.

- ✓ Although a person with a disability might be working, how do they see employment in the future? Do they expect their capabilities to increase or decrease over time, and how will this impact their ability to work?
- ✓ Does any existing health insurance remain in effect and for how long? Is the person with the disability employed by a company that is large enough to offer COBRA? And will these programs coordinate with Medicaid?
- ✓ Does the parents' health insurance provide coverage for a dependent with a disability? For how long?
- ✓ What assets are presently in the name of the person with the

disability (e.g. savings bonds, life insurance, stocks, mutual funds, homes, etc.)?

✓ Is there a possibility of him or her inheriting any money or assets?

For aging adults, be aware of the clause that will have the government look back at a family member's assets up to five years to see if they qualify for government benefits. Long-term care is the leading cause of catastrophic out of pocket costs for families and involves substantial government spending, primarily through Medicaid and Medicare, so planning is necessary in the this area too. Many of our parents think that they can give their assets away to their children, and then they qualify for Medicaid. This is not true. The other area that is confusing is the concept of joint assets. When looking to qualify for Medicaid, all assets of a couple are considered. It doesn't matter if the assets belong to husband or wife; Medicaid considers all assets. There are many elaborate rules in regard to what can and cannot be done in this situation. But there are also many opportunities, if a couple has a family member with a disability. If assets are transferred to a special needs trust, there may be no look back period at all. This is an area that requires specific professional assistance.

Start this step by completing the proper Step 4 Worksheet, called Capture Potential Benefits.   Worksheets appear on the next two pages.

Special Book Offer: Obtain the most current version of these worksheets online at www.protectedtomorrows.com/bookoffer.

Capture Potential Benefits^{TM} - *Disability*

4DIS

Person Requiring Care: _____ Date: _____

Caregiver(s): _____

Government benefits or other disability resources may make up a large part of the required financial support for an individual with special needs, be it a person with a disability or an elderly person needing care. Some are hesitant to tap into these resources, but typically it is due to the lack of knowledge of the programs and the complexity of the applications. These benefits may be essential to the quality of life for your loved one, from residential care, supported employment, health care, and job coaching. This step entails identifying social service, community and government programs that will enhance and support the future care plan of your family members.

What benefit programs is your family member currently receiving?

SSI	SSDI
Medicaid	Medicare
VA	Other _____

Describe the disability of your family member.

Does your family member have any assets in their name?

Checking/Savings	_____	Home	_____
Investments	_____	Car	_____
Life Insurance	_____	Other	_____

Is your family member receiving (or to receive) benefits and working?

Yes.   No. (If No, visit *www.protectedtomorrows.com/bookoffer*)
If Yes, do you report their income to Social Security monthly?
Yes.   No. (If No, visit *www.protectedtomorrows.com/bookoffer*)

Have you made sure that your family member with a disability will not inherit any money from anyone?

Yes, everyone has been informed.
No, we need to do that.
(Visit *www.protectedtomorrows.com/bookoffer*)

Capture Potential Benefits™ - *Senior*

4SR

Person Requiring Care: _____ Date: _____

Caregiver(s): _____

Government benefits or other disability resources may make up a large part of the required financial support for an individual with special needs, be it a person with a disability or an elderly person needing care. Some are hesitant to tap into these resources, but typically it is due to the lack of knowledge of the programs and the complexity of the applications. These benefits may be essential to the quality of life of our loved one, from residential care, supported employment, health care, and job coaching. This step entails identifying social services, community and government programs that will enhance and support the future care plan for our family members.

What benefit programs is your family member currently receiving?

SSI	SSDI
Medicaid	Medicare
VA	Other _____

Describe the disability of your family member.

Is this individual married? | Do they have children?

Yes   No   Yes (How Many? _____)   No

Does your family member have any assets in their name? If so, list them here. If a married couple, list all totals of assets and ownership. Attach a detailed list separately.

Checking/Savings	_____	Home	_____
Investments	_____	Car	_____
Life Insurance	_____	Other	_____

List the monthly income of the individual and their spouse.

Social Security	_____	_____
Pension	_____	_____
Other	_____	_____

Do you feel that there are enough funds to care for the individual, or do you need to pursue government benefits?

There are enough assets.
I need to investigate benefits.
(Visit *www.protectedtomorrows.com/bookoffer*)

Step Five: Document the Wonder™. A family with a person with a disability spends their lifetime finding resources, building self-esteem, joining support groups, and keeping life safe for the person with the disability. A person with a disability does not like change, as there is safety in "sameness". We as parents and caregivers have much of this information in our heads. Share your experiences of your loved one with others. Count yourself among the blessed, because you have been given the privilege of sharing his or her perspective, his or her wonder. Look back on that person's life and reflect on how you have helped him or her over little bits at a time. Acknowledge to yourself that nothing happens overnight. See the progression and how little changes made big differences. When Marcia was diagnosed with a disability, we learned about the disability and the medical solutions over a span of years. We searched out solutions for education and recreation one at a time. This knowledge resided in our brains, but what if something was to happen to one or both of us? Who would know this information unless someone had documented it? Create your own lessons. I learned mine; I'm sure you have learned yours. Share with others the lessons you have learned. It will help you realize just how blessed you are. Since we don't have special powers when we are no longer here, write this information down. It is so important to create a directory of information. We call it **My Special Life**®, which is a book of information that includes everything from basic medical information to daily habits, which will help others maintain a quality of life for your family member with special needs when you are no longer available to be there every day. You can use written form; we also have provided an online system for you to store this information on the Protected Tomorrows website, at www.protectedtomorrows.com.

Start this step by completing the Step 5 Worksheet, called Document the Wonder. The worksheet appears on the next page.

Special Book Offer: Obtain the most current version of this worksheet online at www.protectedtomorrows.com/bookoffer.

PROTECTED TOMORROWS· Document the Wonder™ - All

5

Person Requiring Care: _____ Date: _____

Caregiver(s): _____

It is critical to record important information about your family member including his/her likes/dislikes, routines, habits as well as medical history, so others can continue to step into the caregiving role. This information is key information required by caregivers at residential facilities, as well as teachers, counselors and future guardians. This step is often put off because as caregivers we are overwhelmed with our own lives, let alone the additional caregiving responsibilities. This information can make a big difference in the future quality of life for your loved one. To prepare an entire online record, visit *www.protectedtomorrows.com/bookoffer.*

Category	What I Need to Remember to Share
Residential	
Education	
Employment	
Medical Care	
Social Life	
Religious Activities	
Final Arrangements	
Routines/Habits	

Step Six: Begin the Transition™. This is the step where we shift from the protection of family and state-mandated education benefits to future stages of our family member's life. Or in the case of an elderly parent, we are shifting to finding resources such as adult day care and nursing homes. In most cases, we don't know where to begin. Why would we? We never had to do this before. We have counted on schools and medical professionals to lead the way, and now all of a sudden, we are on our own. The search for information can be overwhelming, so let's count on those who have done this before to share their knowledge with us.

You must identify and evaluate residential, employment, and recreational options for your loved one. The transitional stages of life are extensive and often traumatic. We transition from grammar school to high school. We transition from high school to higher education or life-skills programs. We transition from home to living outside the home. We also transition to assisted living and/or nursing homes. Each of these transitions requires support, solutions, and resources. And patience. How do you begin? You can search for information on our website, www.protectedtomorrows.com. Go to the Special Needs Directory Portal, PTLIVE, to search out tools that will help you build your transition plan. You are not alone. It doesn't have to be a maze of confusing twists and turns. Information is available; you just need to take the step of signing on to look for the first resource. It will get easier after that.

After you have completed the worksheet, start your investigation, one step at a time. Email us or call us if you are feeling lost and alone. We can help.

Start this step by completing the Step 6 Worksheet, called Begin the Transition. The worksheet appears on the next page.

Special Book Offer: Obtain the most current version of this worksheet online at www.protectedtomorrows.com/bookoffer.

Begin the Transition™ - *All*

6

Person Requiring Care: _____ Date: _____

Caregiver(s): _____

Transitions in life occur at many different times. There are childhood transitions, transitions to adulthood, and transitions to senior life. There are probably many more but as caregivers we must be aware of these and prepare for them for the persons we assist in his/her life planning. The best way to prepare is to have good facts, easy access to information, and then it is important to do the necessary legwork to check out the options. This entire process begins with making a list of the options that need to be checked out. Let's start there.

What is the stage of life for your loved one you are planning for?

Early Intervention (ages 0-3)   Adult Years (ages 23-65)
School Years (ages 4-18)   Senior (ages 65-79)
Transition Years (ages 19-22)   Senior (ages 80 and older)

Describe the vision you have for the person you are planning for. Include residential, recreation, wellness and employment wishes.

Identify Options and Explore

Next, go to *www.protectedtomorrows.com/bookoffer*
Find programs related to each of these categories in the zip code area that you are interested in.
List them here with key contact information, as well as the date that you will contact them.

Program Name	*Key Contact*	*Date by which I will research this option*

Step Seven: Fund the Future™. All of the previous steps will now feed into this step, where the financial picture starts to become clearer. Invest in the various resources you have identified in the Future Care Plan. All of the above steps require resources of some sort. Not all are financial, but some are. There may be several opportunities to put a program in place to fund the needs if proper planning is done. Attend advocacy group meetings, such as the complimentary seminars put on by Protected Tomorrows, to learn about how to obtain and maintain benefits and programs that will help. Find other families or friends who have already gone through the same searches. Don't give up. Sometimes, when resources seem scarce, no matter which resource you are looking into, it is easy to feel alone and at risk. Find someone to get you through it. I will say it again. Don't give up. Remember, you can do only the best you can do. Resources come in many sizes, colors, and shapes.

You must take a snapshot as to what assets and liabilities exist to start with. The worksheet for this step will help you do that. Then you will need to fill in the blanks, as the other steps you completed identify areas of concern. This section will address other areas to research to help fill in those financial gaps. You might consider working with a financial professional to assist you in completing the plan for you and your family member.

There are some important areas to investigate to get the whole picture. If the person with the disability has or had a job, investigate their benefits. If you find other personal insurance policies, investigate them as well. Understand the rights of a person with a disability in regard to their financial assets and liabilities:

- ✓ **Disability insurance coverage:** If the person with a disability has and had a job, investigate disability insurance. Employer group or individual disability insurance benefits replace a part of income due to disability. The amount depends on the plan. If he or she has employer group disability coverage, see if it is allowable to increase the coverage and when. If an increase benefit is available during open enrollment without underwriting (medical questions), accept as much coverage as allowed while still working. If he or she has an individual disability plan, check the policy to see if there exists the right to increase the coverage without underwriting. If that right exists, increase the coverage every opportunity available.

✓ **Long term care insurance coverage:** If long term care insurance is offered at work with little or no underwriting, a person with a disability should sign up for as much as possible. The purchase of individual long term care insurance will probably not be an option available to a person with a disability, but you might want to check that out to be sure.

✓ **Life insurance coverage:** Does the person with a disability have life insurance? Does the policy have a disability rider? If it does, recognize that once he/she is no longer able to work, this is an important benefit. The rider will make sure that the life insurance premiums are paid by the insurance company, once the individual is no longer working due to a disability. If the policy has the rider, do not forget to take advantage of it as soon as he or she is eligible.

✓ **Health insurance coverage:** If the company the person with the disability works for offers several plans of health insurance, be sure he or she is on the plan that provides the best coverage for the situation. Typically, employees are able to change plans once a year if the company offers several options. Understand the type of health insurance continuation offered by the employer. Small companies are not required to offer COBRA, but will be required to offer whatever their state requires for small companies. A person with a disability is eligible for COBRA for an extended period of time (not the 18 months you typically hear as offered by COBRA). Also recognize that if a parent has group health insurance coverage with their employer, they may be allowed to keep their dependent with a disability on their group plan. This is an important area to investigate.

✓ **Liabilities:** A person with a disability may have access to credit cards and may want to use them for things they cannot afford due to lack of a full time job. However, that is the opposite of what you would want for him/her. Pay down credit card debt. This is an expense that causes problems later, so it is best eliminated. If the credit cards offer disability coverage, which is reasonably priced, you might look into that, if and only if the debts would be waived upon proof of disability. There are also instances where a person with a disability may have obtained a credit card and built up a balance. Recognize that a person who has a legal guardian typically does not have capacity to own a credit card, as they do not have authority to sign a contract. If that has occurred, you may be able to assist the individual in having the charges waived, since the individual did not have capacity to obtain a credit card. Finally, if a person becomes disabled after incurring college loans, these loans may be able to be waived. Be sure to check out all of these possibilities.

✓ **Income Tax Credits:** Consider teaming up with an accountant to stay informed on the different kinds of tax breaks that apply to people with disabilities and their families—another way of helping your family member get cash in his/her pocket. One example is the Earned Income Tax Credit (EITC)—an anti-poverty program for hard working low-income employees aimed at offsetting the burden of taxes, supplementing low wages, and providing an incentive to work. Working people with disabilities could qualify for EITC.

Tens of thousands of people with disabilities are losing money each year because they are either unaware or do not know how to file for an EITC. Some people might not be filing for the tax credit because they fear they'll lose needed government benefits if he or she receives too much of a refund. People with disabilities receiving SSI or Medicaid cannot have more than $2,000 in assets or income above a certain level, or they might lose funding that affords them food, shelter and could impact their health benefits. Keep in mind the EITC does not count as income in determining eligibility for benefits like cash assistance, Medicaid, food stamps, SSI or public housing.

Specific rules can be found on the IRS website. People with disabilities should turn to specially trained professionals to handle the nuances and refer them to a place that will prepare tax returns free-of–charge.

Start this step by completing the proper Step 7 Worksheet, called Fund the Future. Worksheets appear on the next two pages.

Special Book Offer: Obtain the most current version of these worksheets online at www.protectedtomorrows.com/bookoffer.

Fund the Future™ - *Disabled*

7 DIS

Person Requiring Care: _____ Date: _____

Caregiver(s): _____

After you have a clear picture of the past and future through the previous steps, now is the time to think about the overall financial plan needed to accommodate the vision. If you are planning for a family member with a disability, you might be looking at your own picture to provide for them. Do assets need to be repositioned to provide income? Do additional savings need to be started? Coupled with any government benefit and other programs available, what needs to be adjusted? Are there beneficiary designations that need to be identified and/or modified?

Do you have a current Net Worth statement?

Yes.
No.
(If No, visit *www.protectedtomorrows.com/bookoffer*)

Have you finalized the cash flow needs in Stage 2? If so, how much is needed on a monthly basis to provide sufficient care income now and in the future?

Yes. Total Need: _____
No. Go back to **Step 2 - Create the Future Map**™.

Have you identified all of your life insurance and disability insurance coverage?

I am adequately protected.
I have reviewed my beneficiaries and am confident they are correct.
I need to review my coverage and beneficiary designations.

Have you obtained a current copy of your own Social Security statement so you know how it will impact your family member?

Yes. Amount they may be eligible for on my record. _____
No, I need to that immediately. (Visit *www.ssa.gov*)

Have you met with your financial advisor to implement necessary planning for your family member?

Yes.   No, I need an advisor.
No, I need to call my advisor.   (Visit *www.protectedtomorrows.com/bookoffer*)

Have you already taken care of yourself and all other family members in your planning?

Yes.
No, I need to do so. (Visit *www.protectedtomorrows.com/bookoffer*)

Fund the Future^{TM} - *Senior*

7SR

Person Requiring Care: _____ Date: _____

Caregiver(s): _____

After you have a clear picture of the past and future through the previous steps, now is the time to think about the overall financial plan needed to accommodate the vision. If you are helping an elderly parent, you might be reviewing their own financial status to identify the best way to pay for their care. Do assets need to be repositioned to provide income? Do additional savings need to be started? Coupled with any government benefit and other programs available, what needs to be adjusted? Are there beneficiary designations that need to be identified and/or modified?

Does the individual you are caring for have a current Net Worth statement?

Yes.
No.
(If No, visit *www.protectedtomorrows.com/bookoffer*)

Have you finalized the cash flow needs in Stage 2? If so, how much is needed on a monthly basis to provide sufficient care income now and in the future?

Yes. Total Need: _____
No. Go back to **Step 2 - Create the Future Map**^{TM}.

Have you identified all of his/her life, disability and long term care insurance coverage?

I have investigated the long term care coverage and it is adequate.   Daily Benefit: _____
I am aware of the disability coverage, including whether or not the life insurance policy carries a disability waiver.
I have investigated if any pensions are available.   Monthly Pension: _____
I have investigated if there are any annuities in existence and whether or not they include a nursing home waiver.
I need to make some calls.

Have you met with their financial advisor to implement necessary planning for your family member?

Yes.
No, I need to their advisor.

No, I need an advisor.
(Visit *www.protectedtomorrows.com/bookoffer*)

Step Eight: Review and Renew™. Go over the Future Care Plan annually, in order to accommodate life's inevitable changes. Not only does the Care Plan need review, but the caregiver also needs renewal. Both are equally important components to a Full Life Plan for a person with a disability. Remember, the caregiver's own health and life balance are keys to the overall planning process. Look back to where you were one year ago. Utilize the Step 8 Worksheet to identify how far you have come, where you need to go, and to remind yourself to take care of you, the very important Caregiver.

Start this step by completing the Step 8 Worksheet, called Review and Renew. The worksheet appears on the next page.

Special Book Offer: Obtain the most current version of this worksheet online at www.protectedtomorrows.com/bookoffer.

PROTECTED TOMORROWS® Review and Renew™ - All

8

Person Requiring Care: _____ Date: _____

Caregiver(s): _____

Okay, now it is your turn. This is the time to take a minute and reflect on all you have accomplished. It will help you identify what you still might need to do. Most importantly, it will give you an opportunity to take care of you, the caregiver. As caregivers, we often forget that we need to take care of ourselves. If we don't, we will not be able to take care of anyone else. So let's identify rejuvenation and renewal goals for an important person in this whole planning process, YOU, the caregiver!

List your accomplishments in the planning process to date.

Include not only the number of tasks accomplished, but also identify how it has made a difference in your loved one's life.

GOOD JOB!!!

List the items you would like to work on in the coming year to make the quality of life of your family member even more secure and comfortable.

Identify three things you did for yourself this year to keep yourself rejuvenated.

List three things you plan to do this year for yourself to renew your energy.

What I plan to do for myself   When I promise to do it

1.

2.

3.

So far, our work with families has been very successful. But we recognize now that we are starting to have clients all over the country and all over the world, and we can't possibly be in all these places without expanding our horizons. With this unfilled need as our impetus, we are committed to forming an online presence to help families. Our Process for Protected Tomorrows, as well as our My Special Life program, will be online, accessible to families worldwide. You can find these resources at www.protectedtomorrows.com.

PROTECTED TOMORROWS®

④ CAPTURE Potential Benefits™

Identify and apply for supplemental programs to enhance and supplement the Future Care Plan you have created for your loved one.

③ FILTER the Legal Options™

Evaluate estate solutions, focusing on the various options available through professional legal resources. Implement the steps to take advantage of your decisions.

② CREATE the Future Map™

Identify the options and create a plan to protect your entire family's future in light of your family member's special needs.

① TAKE a Candid Look™

Look honestly and comprehensively at your loved one's future care needs, in light of your own future needs and those of other family members.

Creating the **Future Care Plan**™
for family members with special needs

(5) DOCUMENT the Wonder™

Chronicle and treasure your loved one's special story and gifts so that others can carry forward in building your family member's abilities and self-esteem.

(6) BEGIN the Transition™

Identify and evaluate the future residential, employment, and recreation options for your special needs family member.

(7) FUND the Future™

Utilize financial solutions to complement the **Future Care Plan** designed for your family member's future.

(8) REVIEW and Renew™

Review annually your Future Care Plan to accomodate and address life's inevitable changes.

www.protectedtomorrows.com

Our mission is extensive. It is based upon our passion to find solutions. So often, I've been told by families that the solutions to help their family member are not there, and that the future feels impossible. I don't believe that. I believe that where there is fear, there must be hope. You are not alone.

Our longstanding mission has simply been, and continues to be, to help families with individuals with disabilities in planning for their well-being. We hope to continue to develop new ideas and capabilities and to implement solutions that will be accessible to all families. Our objective is to provide talented and successful people a place—a "think tank" if you will—where they can pool their resources and formulate fresh, new, outside-the-box approaches to problems that have beset us for decades, especially those specific to the lack of residential opportunities and communities for those with disabilities. By doing this, we hope to redraft the business-as-usual solutions offered by government and other organizations and come up with living solutions that will work. My own personal mission statement is to access resources as best I can in order to change the way individuals with disabilities are treated and provided with services. It is the least I can do for my sister Marcia, whose life has so illuminated my own.

But, as one who has experienced having a sister with a disability, and having worked with other families with children with disabilities for many years, I know firsthand that mission statements alone are not enough. It is the love and esteem and dedication and determination that family members bring to these plans that make them work. Therefore, as part of my own personal mission, I have made a promise to myself, and to Marcia's memory, to infuse my work, to the fullest extent possible, with the gifts I have received from Marcia. She gave me many gifts—her laughter, her kindness, her honesty, her courage—but the greatest gift of all for me is that her humanity lives on *through* me and the work I do. It is with Marcia in mind and my gifts from her that the Protected Tomorrows credo has been developed. This credo sets the tone by which all progress will be made, galvanized by the passion and inspiration that Marcia has instilled in me.

Thank you, Marcia.

Thanks, Marcia, Mom and Dad for the inspiration to follow my passion.

WE BELIEVE

Every human being
has a right to live life
to his or her fullest potential.

Desperation and fear
are Mankind's oldest enemies.
A society may fairly be judged
by the extent to which it spares
its most vulnerable citizens
from having to endure them.

OUR HERITAGE

Self-sufficiency is less satisfying
to the soul than caring
for one another.

As Mankind truly is one family,
what benefits any one of us
enhances the lives of us all.
Those of us with greater needs
ennoble their loved ones
by enabling them to feel needed.

OUR GOAL

Make it possible for people
(both the less and more fortunate)
to achieve peace of mind.

To love another
means you can't feel things
are okay until you know
they feel that way.
Your peace of mind
depends on knowing you've helped
bring peace of mind to the other.

OUR BATTLE CRY

Live and help live.

Provide a person
with the means to live
a fuller life and you give more
meaning to yours.

THE KEY

Help those with special needs
attain greater independence and security.

If only the strong were to survive,
wouldn't all of our lives
be greatly diminished?

OUR VALUES

Prepare. Protect. Provide.

The families who count on us
expect nothing less.

OUR SPIRIT

The rock.

We are dedicated,
dependable and enduring.

My Mother's Letter

Mary Anne I'm sure you know all these things I wrote about Marcia!

When the twins were born & I was told the one had a problem, I wondered how I could cope. But somehow I did, we all did!

Having Marcia taught me so many things. She never complained about all her hardships, but down deep I know she would've liked to be "normal" like her siblings.

She taught me to accept people as they are.

When she lived in the "Big" facility, things sometimes were disrupted in her room by other residents. If I made any comments about this, her answer always was "They didn't know any different." She always was glad to have company.

Marcia always liked to have things neat! mostly so she could find them easily. Her glasses were very important to her. They had to be in the same place at all times. Because of her considered being legally blind made things doubly hard.

She liked to be busy. Some of her aids at the 16 bed facility were great, others tried to do as little as possible. That's the way of human nature. She got along with all that worked there. One of her favorite people there was the cook, Clara. If she couldn't come to work because of illness that was a catastrophe in Marcia's Day. Clara was a fun person. But on St. church service she made ... she did take her up to the altar to specially pray for her friend. Her teacher at Day training always had good things to say about Marcia.

108

Before she died, I think she was ~~being~~ living the best-being of her life. Her seizures were controlled really well & enjoyed her home and the residential also. Her comment was she was so lucky to have 2 homes.

I think the last year before she died, she became much more independent. If she could do a task, she really did not want help.

There were many health problems but she always acted well. One of her worst things was to go to the hospital, and she had many of those days.

I know Marcia is at peace with the Lord, but somehow I still worry about her.

She has left us 2½ yrs ago and I can't seem to get on with my life without her. I know I must, but how can one say it is easier as time goes on. You could miss her any less. At the family gatherings for me is difficult. That was one of the things she loved.

109

SPECIAL OFFER!

Special Bonus Program for The Gift I was Given readers!

The online Process for Protected Tomorrows™ Program
walks you through a step-by-step planning system.

Find the Ah Ha! of your own personal caregiving journey.

Come visit us at:

www.protectedtomorrows.com/bookoffer

Sign up for the free Protected Tomorrows Newsletter,
Protected Tomorrows Today
Stay up to date with the many services available to you and your
family

www.protectedtomorrows.com

For information about a Protected Tomorrows workshop or
to request Mary Anne Ehlert to speak at your conference, reach us at:
Protected Tomorrows
LifeCare Center
103 Schelter Road
Lincolnshire, IL 60069
Telephone (847) 522-8086

BUY A SHARE OF THE FUTURE IN YOUR COMMUNITY

These certificates make great holiday, graduation and birthday gifts that can be personalized with the recipient's name. The cost of one S.H.A.R.E. or one square foot is $54.17. The personalized certificate is suitable for framing and will state the number of shares purchased and the amount of each share, as well as the recipient's name. The home that you participate in "building" will last for many years and will continue to grow in value.

Here is a sample SHARE certificate:

YES, I WOULD LIKE TO HELP!

I support the work that Habitat for Humanity does and I want to be part of the excitement! As a donor, I will receive periodic updates on your construction activities but, more importantly, I know my gift will help a family in our community realize the dream of homeownership. **I would like to SHARE in your efforts against substandard housing in my community!** *(Please print below)*

PLEASE SEND ME _____ SHARES at $54.17 EACH = $ $_____

In Honor Of: _____

Occasion: (Circle One)   HOLIDAY   BIRTHDAY   ANNIVERSARY

      OTHER: _____

Address of Recipient: _____

Gift From: _____ *Donor Address:* _____

Donor Email: _____

I AM ENCLOSING A CHECK FOR $ $_____ PAYABLE TO HABITAT FOR HUMANITY OR PLEASE CHARGE MY VISA OR MASTERCARD *(CIRCLE ONE)*

Card Number _____ Expiration Date: _____

Name as it appears on Credit Card _____ Charge Amount $ _____

Signature _____

Billing Address _____

Telephone # Day _____ Eve _____

PLEASE NOTE: Your contribution is tax-deductible to the fullest extent allowed by law.
Habitat for Humanity • P.O. Box 1443 • Newport News, VA 23601 • 757-596-5553
www.HelpHabitatforHumanity.org